CAREER CRITTERS

An Innovative Career-Exploration Program
for Grades 1–2

By
ARDEN MARTENZ
&
KEN SMITH

Illustrated by
HARRY NORCROSS

revised/reprinted 2004
copyright © 1997
mar*co products, inc.

Published by **mar*co products, inc.**
1443 Old York Road, Warminster, PA 18974
1-800-448-2197

Library of Congress Catalog Card Number: 97-073414
ISBN: 1-57543-052-5
Printed in the U.S.A.

TABLE OF CONTENTS

INTRODUCTION

Career Critters is a creative career-awareness program for early primary students. Each lesson includes a leader's guide and a reproducible booklet with a story and activity pages. The program's purpose is to:

- acquaint young students with many different careers
- help young students gain self-knowledge
- emphasize the importance of work in relation to society's needs

The program includes 15 lessons, one for each career cluster. The career clusters are identified on the cover of each student booklet. It is not necessary to present the booklets in any particular order, or even to present all of them. Facilitators should decide how many of the lessons are appropriate for their particular groups.

USING PUPPETS:

Career Critters can be presented with or without puppets. Seven animals are featured in the stories, and seven stick puppets patterns are included with the program (pages 191-199).

If you choose to use the stick puppets, make the ones you need before you begin the lesson. You will find directions on page 192. If you are using commercial puppets or plush animals, you will need to obtain a whale, squirrel, raccoon, skunk, bear, donkey, and husky dog.

INVOLVING THE STUDENTS IN THE PRESENTATION:

At the beginning of each lesson, assign a student to assume the role of each of the characters in the story. If you are using puppets, give each student the puppet that matches his/her assigned character. Ask these students to sit near you.

The questions found in the leader's guide should be asked after each page of the story is read. The students portraying the characters in the story then have the opportunity to interact with one another.

Other questions are asked of students who are *not* holding the puppets, so everyone has an opportunity to participate in the lesson.

PARENT LETTER:

A reproducible *Parent Letter* is found on page 9. This letter explains the purpose of the program. The letter should be sent home to parents before the program begins. Parents will then be aware of the program and its purpose and be able to reinforce the concepts at home.

TIME REQUIRED:

Each lesson takes between 30 and 40 minutes, depending upon the format used and how well the students express themselves.

PREPARING FOR THE PRESENTATION:

Select the desired lesson and reproduce the student pages. The pages are laid out so that when reproduced, they can be made into 8-page booklets. These user-friendly booklets should be prepared before the lesson is presented. The students will also need pencils and crayons or markers.

Dear Parent:

Education plays an important part in preparing children for their future careers. In a short time, your child's class will be learning about different occupations. This is not an attempt to persuade children to choose careers, but to make them aware of this important aspect of life and society.

Work will someday be an important part of your child's life. The more information children have about careers, the better prepared they will be to make choices when the time comes. Another important part of this program is helping children realize that schooling, even at this grade level, is necessary for their future. This realization affects attitudes toward work, and those attitudes play an essential part in your child's achievements now and as an adult.

Your child will be bringing home career information that was presented in class. Please look over these booklets and add any information you can about your job, family members' jobs, or acquaintances' jobs that relate to the topic being presented. Your participation will give your child a better understanding of the relationship between school and work.

Thank you for your cooperation.

Yours truly,

AGRICULTURAL AND NATURAL RESOURCES JOBS

AGRICULTURAL AND NATURAL RESOURCES JOBS
LEADER'S GUIDE

If you are using puppets, select the raccoon, skunk, bear, and squirrel.

Introduce the lesson by telling the students they will be learning about some jobs they see on television, in the movies, at tree nurseries, on farms, and read about in books.

Distribute the student booklets and pencils. Have the students complete the first page. Tell the students that people who make their living growing vegetables, raising animals, growing trees, growing flowers, mining, and harvesting lumber have jobs in *Agriculture and Natural Resources*. (If necessary, explain the difference between *agriculture* and *natural resources*.)

Have the students turn to the second page. Read the first part of the page with the students. When naming the four jobs listed on the page, have the students tell how each relates to agriculture or natural resources.

Then ask the students to name some other jobs that involve agriculture and natural resources. Write the appropriate answers on the chalkboard. Some examples could be: *cowhand, butcher, dairy farmer, landscaper, lumberjack, oil rig worker.* Then have the students select three *Agricultural and Natural Resources Jobs* and write them on the lines on the page. Read the last sentences on the page with the students.

Tell the students there will be several animal characters in the story and that some of the students will pretend to be the animal characters. Select four students to pretend to be the animal characters. (The skunk and squirrel should be boys, and the raccoon and bear should be girls.) If you are using puppets, give each of the chosen students his/her puppet. Tell these students to sit near you during the lesson and that they will be involved in the story at certain times. They will be involved by answering questions. Explain that when you want them to answer a question, you will call them by the name of the animal in the story.

Have the students look at page 3. Read the text with the students. When you have finished reading, ask the following questions:

For the student holding the raccoon puppet:

- *Rita, how did you feel when you heard the rooster crowing?*
- *How did you feel about doing your morning chore?*

For the rest of the students:

- *How many different jobs can you name that have something to do with farms?*

Have the students turn to page 4. Read the text with the students. When you have finished reading, ask the following questions:

For the student holding the skunk puppet:

- *Sidney, if you grew your very own pumpkin, what would you do with it?*

For the rest of the students:

- *What would be the hardest thing about being a farmer?*
- *What would be the best thing about being a farmer?*

Have the students look at page 5. Read the text with the students. When you have finished reading, ask the following questions:

For the student holding the bear puppet:

- *Bonnie, why were you wearing a netting that covered your head? (for protection from the bees.)*
- *How do you feel about tending bees?*

For the student holding the raccoon puppet:

- *Rita, why were you glad Bonnie offered you some honey?*

For the rest of the students:

- *How many jobs can you name that have something to do with bees?*
- *What would be the hardest thing about being a beekeeper?*
- *What would be the best thing about being a beekeeper?*

CAREER CRITTERS © MAR∗CO PRODUCTS, INC. 1-800-448-2197

Have the students turn to page 6. Read the text with the students. When you have finished reading, ask the following questions:

For the student holding the squirrel puppet:

- *Sammy, why do you think your uncle chose to be a gardener?*
- *How did you feel when you were helping your uncle work in the garden?*

For the student holding the raccoon puppet:

- *Rita, what do you think you have to remember when picking tomatoes?*

For the rest of the students:

- *How many jobs can you name that have something to do with gardens?*
- *What would be the hardest thing about being a gardener?*
- *What would be the best thing about being a gardener?*

If puppets were used in the lesson, collect them from the students.

Give the students crayons or markers and have them complete the activities on pages 7 and 8. If they finish before the allotted time has elapsed, tell them they may color the pictures on other pages.

Conclude the lesson by having the students share their activity pages with the class. Then tell the students they may take their booklets home to share with their parents.

AGRICULTURAL AND NATURAL RESOURCES JOBS

NAME

TEACHER

GRADE

1

Grown-ups do many different kinds of jobs. **Agricultural Jobs** have to do with raising plants or animals for food. **Natural Resources Jobs** can be drilling for oil or cutting trees for lumber.

Four **Agricultural and Natural Resources Jobs** are:

1. Beekeeper

2. Farmer

3. Gardener

4. Miner

Three more **Agricultural and Natural Resources Jobs** are:

1. _____

2. _____

3. _____

In this booklet, a raccoon named Rita tells about her life on the farm. As she does her morning chore, Rita introduces us to some of the different jobs on the farm where she lives.

FARMING FOR FOOD

Rita Raccoon wakes up to the sound of a rooster crowing. She must get up early to do her morning chore. She gets dressed quickly, goes downstairs, and heads out of her house. The chill of the morning air helps her wake up. She walks to the barn.

CAREER CRITTERS: AGRICULTURAL AND NATURAL RESOURCES JOBS—STUDENT BOOKLET
© 1996 MAR∗CO PRODUCTS, INC. 1-800-448-2197

As Rita enters the barn, she sees Sidney Skunk. Sidney's uncle is busy putting oil in the tractor. When Sidney sees Rita, he says, "Hi, Rita!"

"Where are you working today?" asks Rita. Sidney tells her they are plowing the west fields. They are getting the fields ready for planting. This year, they are going to grow pumpkins. Rita and Sidney agree that they are going to grow the biggest pumpkins of all.

CAREER CRITTERS: AGRICULTURAL AND NATURAL RESOURCES JOBS—STUDENT BOOKLET
© 1996 MAR∗CO PRODUCTS, INC. 1-800-448-2197

Rita turns around to see Bonnie Bear. Bonnie is wearing a white canvas outfit. A hat with netting covers her entire head. "Are you and your mom tending the bees today?" asks Rita.

"That's right," replies Bonnie. "We're going to harvest the honey. Would you like some when I'm finished?"

"Like some?" answers Rita. "I'd love some! Your bees make the sweetest honey of all."

CAREER CRITTERS: AGRICULTURAL AND NATURAL RESOURCES JOBS—STUDENT BOOKLET
© 1996 MAR★CO PRODUCTS, INC. 1-800-448-2197

Rita grabs a basket and leaves the barn to do her morning chore. As she enters the garden, she sees Sammy Squirrel. Sammy is the gardener's nephew. Sammy says, "Hi, Rita! Are you here to pick some tomatoes?"

"Yes," answers Rita. As she picks the tomatoes, Sammy and his uncle are pulling weeds and staking the tomato plants. Rita loves working on the farm.

WHAT WOULD YOU RAISE?

Pretend you are a farmer. Circle the pictures of the plants or animals you would have on your farm.

7

Right now, I am _____ years old. This is a picture of me doing an **Agricultural and Natural Resources Job**. Right now, this is what I think I might like to do.

BUT I CAN ALWAYS CHANGE MY MIND!

CAREER CRITTERS: AGRICULTURAL AND NATURAL RESOURCES JOBS—STUDENT BOOKLET
© 1996 MAR∗CO PRODUCTS, INC. 1-800-448-2197

BUSINESS
AND
OFFICE
JOBS

BUSINESS AND OFFICE JOBS
LEADER'S GUIDE

If you are using puppets, select the Husky dog, whale, bear, and squirrel.

Introduce the lesson by telling the students they will be learning about some jobs they see on television, in the movies, in their community, and read about in books.

Distribute the student booklets and pencils. Have the students complete the first page. Tell the students that people who make a living counting money, writing contracts, typing letters, and making business decisions have jobs in *Business and Offices*.

Have the students turn to the second page. Read the first part of the page with the students. When naming the four jobs listed on the page, have the students tell how each one helps the business or office.

Then ask the students to name some other jobs that involve *Business and Offices*. Write the appropriate answers on the chalkboard. Some examples could be: *computer operator, manager, cashier, accountant.* Have the students select three *Business and Office Jobs* and write them on the lines on the page. Read the last sentences on the page with the students.

Tell the students there will be several animal characters in the story and that some of the students will pretend to be the animal characters. (The whale and bear should be boys, and the Husky dog and squirrel should be girls.) If you are using puppets, give each of the chosen students his/her puppet. Tell these students to sit near you during the lesson and that they will be involved in the story at certain times.

Have the students look at page 3. Read the text with the students. When you have finished reading, ask the following questions:

For the student holding the Husky dog puppet:

- *Hanna, why is this a special morning?*
- *How did you feel when you heard you were going to visit an office?*

For the student holding the whale puppet:

- *Waldo, office workers spend a lot of time indoors. Would you like to do that?*

For the rest of the students:

- *How many different jobs can you name that have something to do with offices?*

Have the students turn to page 4. Read the text with the students. When you have finished reading, ask the following questions:

For the student holding the squirrel puppet:

- *Shanna, why is it important for your aunt to be cheerful and polite to people who come into the building? (to make them feel welcome)*

For the rest of the students:

- *What would be the hardest thing about being a receptionist?*
- *What would be the best thing about being a receptionist?*

Have the students look at page 5. Read the text with the students. When you have finished reading, ask the following questions:

For the student holding the bear puppet:

- *Bono, what is the best thing about being a secretary?*
- *How did you feel when you heard that your father helped Waldo's father get things done?*

For the rest of the students:

- *How many jobs can you name that have something to do with helping others get things done?*
- *What would be the hardest thing about being a secretary?*
- *What would be the best thing about being a secretary?*

Have the students turn to page 6. Read the text with the students. When you have finished reading, ask the following questions:

For the student holding the whale puppet:

- *Waldo, why do you think your father has to be good at math? (He does not want to make errors.)*
- *Why do you think your father's job is important?*

For the student holding the Husky dog puppet:

- *Why do you think you would like to be a bookkeeper?*

For the rest of the students:

- *How many jobs can you name that have to do with counting money?*
- *What would be the hardest thing about being a bookkeeper?*
- *What would be the best thing about being a bookkeeper?*

If puppets were used in the lesson, collect them from the students.

Give the students crayons or markers and have them complete the activities on pages 7 and 8. If they finish before the allotted time has elapsed, tell them they may color the pictures on other pages.

Conclude the lesson by having the students share their activity pages with the class. Then tell the students they may take their booklets home to share with their parents.

BUSINESS AND OFFICE JOBS

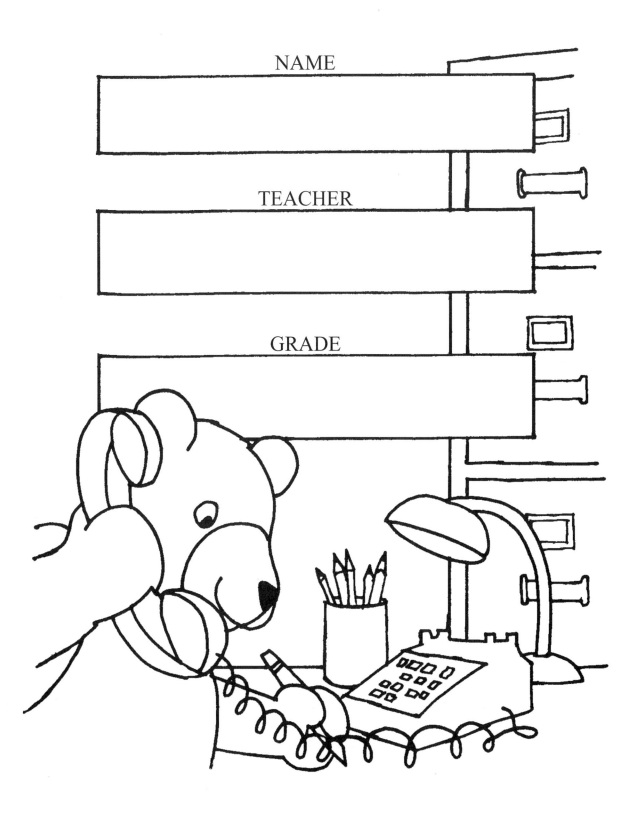

NAME

TEACHER

GRADE

CAREER CRITTERS: BUSINESS AND OFFICE JOBS—STUDENT BOOKLET
© 1996 MAR∗CO PRODUCTS, INC. 1-800-448-2197

Have you ever looked at a building and wondered what the grown-ups inside the building were doing? They might be working at their desks, answering telephones, or working at their computers. These and other jobs are called **Business and Office Jobs.**

Four **Business and Office Jobs** are:

1. Receptionist

2. Business Owner

3. Secretary

4. Bookkeeper

Three more **Business and Office Jobs** are:

1. _____

2. _____

3. _____

In this booklet, a Husky dog named Hanna visits Waldo Whale's father at his office. She learns that people do many different jobs in an office building.

OFFICE OUTING

Hanna Husky wakes up on a very special morning. Today is Career-Awareness Day, and Hanna is going to the office where Waldo Whale's father works. By doing this, Hanna can learn what it would be like to work in an office. Hanna has been looking forward to this day, and she is very excited. She gets out of bed, gets dressed, and hurries out the door.

CAREER CRITTERS: BUSINESS AND OFFICE JOBS—STUDENT BOOKLET
© 1996 MAR∗CO PRODUCTS, INC. 1-800-448-2197

When Hanna and Waldo's father arrive at the office building, they are greeted by the receptionist. The receptionist is Shanna Squirrel's aunt. She is very friendly and welcomes Hanna to the workplace. She tells Hanna that her job is to direct visitors to where they want to go and to the person they are supposed to meet in the building. Shanna's aunt loves her job because she helps others.

4

Hanna and Waldo's father ride the elevator to the floor where his office is located. As they walk toward the office, Hanna notices someone seated at a desk outside Waldo's father's office. Waldo's father tells Hanna the person at the desk is his secretary. Waldo's father introduces Hanna to his secretary, Mr. Bear. The secretary tells Hanna that he has a son, Bono. Bono's father is very friendly. He says he enjoys helping Waldo's father get things done.

CAREER CRITTERS: BUSINESS AND OFFICE JOBS—STUDENT BOOKLET
© 1996 MAR∗CO PRODUCTS, INC. 1-800-448-2197

Waldo's father tells Hanna he is a bookkeeper. It is his job to keep track of the money paid to the business and the money the business spends. He tells Hanna it is very important for a business to make more money than it spends.

As a bookkeeper, Waldo's father gives the owner of the business the information she needs to make important decisions about money. Hanna thinks Waldo's father's job is very important. Some day, she would like to be a bookkeeper, too.

6

WHAT DO YOU FIND IN AN OFFICE?

Circle the pictures of things or people you would find in an office building. Put an ✗ over the things or people you would **not** find in an office building.

Right now, I am _____ years old. This is a picture of me doing a **Business and Office Job**. Right now, this is what I think I would like to do.

BUT I CAN ALWAYS CHANGE MY MIND!

COMMUNICATION
AND
MEDIA
JOBS

COMMUNICATION AND MEDIA JOBS
LEADER'S GUIDE

If you are using puppets, select the squirrel, raccoon, donkey, and whale.

Introduce the lesson by telling the students that they will be learning about some jobs in which people give information to other people either by talking with them or by showing them pictures. They may talk with them over the telephone or on television or through the computer. They may show them pictures in a video, on television, in the movies, in a magazine, or on the computer. *Communication* is information, and *media* are the ways people get information. People use different kinds of media to communicate with others.

Distribute the booklets and pencils and have the students complete the first page.

Have the students turn to the second page. Read the first part of the page with the students. When naming the four jobs listed on the page, tell the students that they will be learning about these jobs in their booklets.

Then ask the students to name some other jobs that involve *Communication and Media*. Write the appropriate answers on the chalkboard. Some examples could be: *photographer, telephone operator, illustrator, filmmaker, newspaper reporter, radio disc jockey, computer programmer.* For each job mentioned, have the students tell how people communicate through it and what media are used. Next, have the students select three *Communication and Media Jobs* and write them on the lines on the page. Read the last sentence on the page with the students.

Tell the students there will be several animal characters in the story and that some of the students will pretend to be the animal characters. (The squirrel and donkey should be boys, and the raccoon and whale should be girls.) If you are using puppets, give each of the chosen students his/her puppet. Tell these students to sit near you during the lesson and that they will be involved in the story at certain times.

Have the students look at page 3. Read the text with the students. When you have finished reading, ask the following questions:

For the student holding the squirrel puppet:

- *Sammy, do you think anyone will answer your e-mail?*
- *What other kinds of messages might be e-mailed?*

Have the students turn to page 4. Read the text with the students. When you have finished reading, ask the following questions:

For the student holding the whale puppet:

- *Winnie, why do you think so many people would like to be TV announcers? (People will know who you are and a you will make a lot of money.)*

For the student holding the raccoon puppet:

- *Rita, what do you think would be the hardest thing for an air traffic controller to do?*

For the rest of the students:

- *Which TV announcer would you like to be? Why?*
- *What do you think it would be like to be an air traffic controller in NAME YOUR HOMETOWN? (If there is no airport near you, name the nearest large city.)*

Have the students look at page 5. Read the text with the students. When you have finished reading, ask the following questions:

For the student holding the donkey puppet:

- *Danny, in order to do this job the right way, what must a 911 dispatcher do? (Listen carefully, get information, think fast.)*

For the rest of the students:

- *What do you think might upset a 911 dispatcher?*

Have the students turn to page 6. Read the text with the students. When you have finished reading, ask the following questions:

For the student holding the squirrel puppet:

- *Sammy, what would be the hardest thing about being a line installer?*
- *What would be the best thing about being a line installer?*

For the rest of the students:

- *Do you think there will be jobs in communication and media when you grow up? Why or why not?*
- *If you had to be either a line installer, air traffic controller, 911 dispatcher, or TV announcer, which job would you pick first? Which job would you pick last? Why?*

If puppets were used in the lesson, collect them from the students.

Give the students crayons or markers and have them complete the activities on pages 7 and 8. If they finish before the allotted time has elapsed, tell them they may color the pictures on other pages. When the students have finished, have them share their activity pages with the class.

Conclude the lesson by telling the students that you will name six different *Communication and Media Jobs*. Name the six jobs and designate a section of the room for each job. Tell the students to go to the section of the room designated for the job that interests them most. When every student has chosen a job, ask the students why they believe the job most students selected was more popular than the others.

Tell the students they may take their booklets home to share with their parents.

COMMUNICATION AND MEDIA JOBS

NAME

TEACHER

GRADE

1

Computers, television, newspapers, telephones, movies, radio, letters, and books are all ways that people give and get information. These ways of communicating are called *media*. All of them have jobs for many people. These jobs are called **Communication and Media Jobs.**

Four **Communication and Media Jobs** are:

1. Line Installer

2. TV Announcer

3. Dispatcher

4. Air Traffic Controller

Three more **Communication and Media Jobs** are:

1. _____

2. _____

3. _____

In this booklet, a squirrel named Sammy learns about communication jobs through his computer.

SAMMY SURFS THE NET

Sammy Squirrel was sitting at his computer. He was hoping for some e-mail, but there was none. So Sammy decided to surf the Internet.

Sammy decided he would contact other kids about communication jobs. First, he decided to e-mail Danny Donkey with this message: Do you know anyone with a communication job? Sammy sent the same message to Winnie Whale and Rita Raccoon.

CAREER CRITTERS: COMMUNICATION AND MEDIA JOBS—STUDENT BOOKLET
© 1996 MAR✱CO PRODUCTS, INC. 1-800-448-2197

The next day, Sammy turned on his computer and went straight to the Internet. The message was there: You have mail. One message was from Winnie Whale. It said: My aunt is a TV announcer. She tells people all the news of the day.

The next message was from Rita Raccoon. She said: My uncle is an air traffic controller at the airport. He watches a radar screen so he can help planes land safely.

4

The last message was from Danny Donkey. He said: My mom is a dispatcher for 911. She gets calls when people are in trouble. She has to keep them calm and get as much information as she can in order to send the right people to help them. It is important to remember that you call 911 only in an emergency.

CAREER CRITTERS: COMMUNICATION AND MEDIA JOBS—STUDENT BOOKLET
© 1996 MAR✳CO PRODUCTS, INC. 1-800-448-2197

"Time for bed," Sammy's mother called. Sammy shut off his computer. He went to bed, but he couldn't sleep. He was thinking about all of the different communication jobs. His dad has one. He is a line installer. His dad put in the telephone lines that let Sammy work and play on his computer. There are other communication jobs, too. Newspaper reporter, filmmaker, radio disc jockey, computer programmer, photographer, advertising copywriter, telephone oper..a..t..or....... Sammy was asleep.

6

COLOR YOUR FEELINGS

All of these things have to do with some kind of communication or media job. Color the square red if this is something you like doing. Color the square green if this is something you do not mind doing. Color the square blue if this is something you do **not** like doing.

I like to:

☐ 1. talk with people

☐ 2. take pictures with a camera

☐ 3. help people

☐ 4. pay attention to what I am doing

☐ 5. draw pictures

CAREER CRITTERS: COMMUNICATION AND MEDIA JOBS—STUDENT BOOKLET
© 1996 MAR✳CO PRODUCTS, INC. 1-800-448-2197

Right now, I am _____ years old. This is a picture of me doing a **Communication and Media Job.** Right now, this is what I think I might like to do.

BUT I CAN ALWAYS CHANGE MY MIND!

CAREER CRITTERS: COMMUNICATION AND MEDIA JOBS—STUDENT BOOKLET
© 1996 MAR∗CO PRODUCTS, INC. 1-800-448-2197

CONSTRUCTION JOBS

CONSTRUCTION JOBS
LEADER'S GUIDE

If you are using puppets, select the donkey, raccoon, bear, and squirrel.

Introduce the lesson by telling the students they will be learning about some jobs they might see people doing while they are riding in a car or walking down a street.

Distribute the student booklets and pencils. Have the students complete the first page. Tell the students that people who make a living building houses, stores, apartment buildings, hospitals, and roads have jobs in *Construction*.

Have the students turn to the second page. Read the first part of the page with the students. When naming the four jobs listed on the page, have the students tell how each job helps make something.

Then ask the students to name some other jobs that involve *Construction*. Write the appropriate answers on the chalkboard. Some examples could be: *plumber, roofer, bricklayer, architect, heavy-equipment operator.* Next, have the students select three *Construction Jobs* and write them on the lines on the page. Read the last sentences on the page with the students.

Tell the students there will be several animal characters in the story and that some of the students will pretend to be the animal characters. (The donkey and squirrel should be boys, and the raccoon and bear should be girls.) If you are using puppets, give each of the chosen students his/her puppet. Tell these students to sit near you during the lesson and that they will be involved in the story at certain times.

Have the students look at page 3. Read the text with the students. When you have finished reading, ask the following questions:

For the student holding the donkey puppet:

- *Danny, why did someone tell you not to come any closer? (Construction sites can be dangerous, and Danny could have been hurt.)*

For the rest of the students:

- *What are some good reasons for not playing around a construction site?*

Have the students turn to page 4. Read the text with the students. Define the word *supervisor*. When you have finished reading, ask the following questions:

For the student holding the raccoon puppet:

- *Rita, what did your mother have to learn before becoming a construction supervisor? (She needed to learn everything about constructing a building.)*

For the rest of the students:

- *What would be the hardest thing about being a supervisor?*
- *What would be the best thing about being a supervisor?*

Have the students look at page 5. Read the text with the students. When you have finished reading, ask the following questions:

For the student holding the squirrel puppet:

- *Sammy, how does it make you feel to know a neighbor who has an important job?*

For the rest of the students:

- *What would be the hardest thing about being a mason?*
- *What would be the best thing about being a mason?*

Have the students turn to page 6. Read the text with the students. When you have finished reading, ask the following questions:

For the student holding the bear puppet:

- *Bonnie, what could happen if your aunt did not measure carefully? (The building would be crooked.)*

For the student holding the donkey puppet:

- *Danny, how did you feel when you heard that you could visit the construction site another day?*

For the rest of the students:

- *How many jobs can you name that have to do with using wood?*
- *What would be the hardest thing about being a carpenter?*
- *What would be the best thing about being a carpenter?*

If puppets were used in the lesson, collect them from the students.

Give the students crayons or markers and have them complete the activities on pages 7 and 8. If they finish before the allotted time has elapsed, tell them they may color the pictures on other pages.

Conclude the lesson by having the students share their activity pages with the class. Then tell the students they may take their booklets home to share with their parents.

CONSTRUCTION JOBS

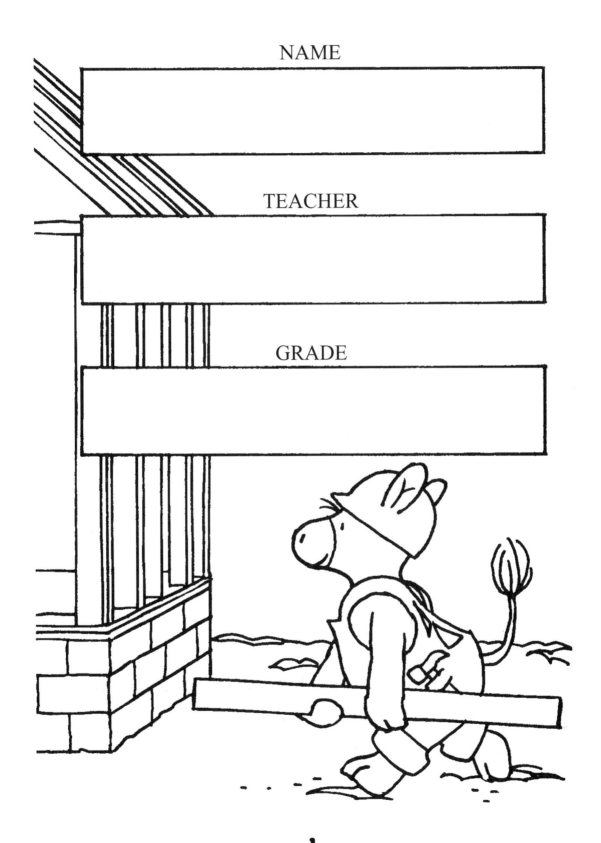

NAME

TEACHER

GRADE

1

Have you ever wondered how the pipes were put into your house? Have you ever wished you could drive a backhoe? These jobs and others have to do with building houses, stores, offices, and roads. These are **Construction Jobs.**

Four **Construction Jobs** are:

1. Construction Supervisor

2. Carpenter

3. Mason

4. Electrician

Three more **Construction Jobs** are:

1. _____

2. _____

3. _____

In this booklet, a donkey named Danny goes to a construction site. While he is there, he discovers that many different jobs are needed to build a building.

CAREER CRITTERS: CONSTRUCTION JOBS—STUDENT BOOKLET
© 1996 MAR∗CO PRODUCTS, INC. 1-800-448-2197

BUILDING BUILDINGS

Danny Donkey overheard his father say that a new
building was being built on their street. Danny
thought it would be fun to watch the workers, so he
walked down the street until he saw where the new
building was being built. There were so many
workers! Danny didn't know which one to watch
first. As Danny walked toward the workers, he heard
a voice say, "Hey kid, don't come any closer!"

The voice was that of the site supervisor. She is Rita Raccoon's mother. She told Danny that she is in charge of the construction workers, and that a construction site was not a safe place for children. Danny was disappointed. All he wanted to do was watch. Rita's mother understood and decided to help him. She said she would give him a tour of the site. "Great!" said Danny.

CAREER CRITTERS: CONSTRUCTION JOBS—STUDENT BOOKLET
© 1996 MAR✳CO PRODUCTS, INC. 1-800-448-2197

The first worker Rita's mother introduced to Danny was Sammy Squirrel's neighbor. He is a mason. He told Danny that a mason's job is to lay the foundation for the building. The foundation is the bottom of the building. The foundation must be very strong, because the whole building rests upon it. Danny thought that being a mason and laying the foundation was a very important construction job.

Then Danny met Bonnie Bear's aunt. She is a carpenter. Bonnie's aunt told Danny that her job is to make the frame of the building. She said that when she is finished, electricians, bricklayers, plumbers, and other workers would be able to do their jobs.

Rita's mother's beeper sounded. She answered it, and said she had to go back to work. It was time for Danny to leave, but Rita's mother told him he could come back another day. Danny left, feeling great.

BUILD YOUR OWN BUILDING

Draw a picture of any kind of building that you would like to build.

Right now, I am _____ years old. This is a picture of me doing a **Construction Job.** Right now, this is what I think I might like to do.

BUT I CAN ALWAYS CHANGE MY MIND!

CONSUMER
EDUCATION
AND
HOMEMAKING
JOBS

CONSUMER-EDUCATION AND HOMEMAKING JOBS
LEADER'S GUIDE

If you are using puppets, select the whale, skunk, raccoon, and bear.

Introduce the lesson by telling the students they will be learning about some jobs that help people and make them happy.

Distribute the student booklets and pencils. Have the students complete the first page.

Have the students turn to the second page. Read the first part of the page with the students. When naming the four jobs listed on the page, have the students tell how each one helps people.

Then ask the students to name some other jobs that involve *Consumer-Education and Homemaking*. Write the appropriate answers on the chalkboard. Tell them to think of things to make life better. Tell them that some of these jobs may also be found in other booklets. Some examples could be: *dietitian, upholsterer, comparison shopper, food editor, dressmaker, dry cleaner.* Next, have the students select three *Consumer-Education and Homemaking Jobs* and write them on the lines on the page. Read the last sentence on the page with the students.

Tell the students there will be several animal characters in the story and that some of the students will pretend to be the animal characters. (The raccoon and whale should be boys, and the skunk and bear should be girls.) If you are using puppets, give each of the chosen students his/her puppet. Tell these students to sit near you during the lesson and that they will be involved in the story at certain times.

Have the students look at page 3. Read the text with the students. When you have finished reading, ask the following questions:

For student holding the raccoon puppet:

• *Raul, when you help around the house, which job do you like most?*

For the rest of the students:

- *Why is homemaking an important job? (A homemaker keeps a home and family running smoothly.)*
- *If a homemaker could not read, what might happen?*
- *If a homemaker could not write, what might happen?*
- *If a homemaker could not do math, what might happen?*

Have the students turn to page 4. Read the text with the students. When you have finished reading, ask the following questions:

For the student holding the skunk puppet:

- *Selena, do you think your mom works in an office most of the time. Or does she go to people's homes?*

For the rest of the students:

- *What new products might Selena's mom tell people to use to make their lives better?*

Have the students look at page 5. Read the text with the students. When you have finished reading, ask the following questions:

For the student holding the bear puppet:

- *Bonnie, what things might your mom look for to make sure food is safe to eat? (mold, bruises, proper packaging, etc.)*

For the rest of the students:

- *Why is this job important?*
- *Bonnie's mother works for a food company. Who else could she work for as a food inspector? (the government)*

Have the students turn to page 6. Read the text with the students. When you have finished reading, ask the following questions:

For the student holding the whale puppet:

- *Waldo, what time do you think your uncle would have to get up in the morning to have breakfast ready for the sailors by 6 o'clock?*

For the rest of the students:

- *Waldo's uncle cooks for the sailors in the Navy. Can you think of any other places, besides restaurants, where people cook for large groups? (school cafeterias, cafeterias in businesses)*

If puppets were used in the lesson, collect them from the students.

Give the students crayons or markers. Tell them that homemakers must be able to do math. Have them complete the problems on page 7 and the activity on page 8. If they finish before the allotted time has elapsed, tell them they may color the pictures on other pages.

Conclude the lesson by having the students share their activity pages with the class. Then tell the students they may take their booklets home to share with their parents.

CONSUMER-EDUCATION
AND
HOMEMAKING JOBS

NAME

TEACHER

GRADE

1

This booklet tells about jobs that have to do with things people use in their homes. You may be surprised to find that many jobs have to do with things you do or use every day. These are **Consumer-Education and Homemaking Jobs**. Some of these jobs have long names, so you may learn some new words.

Four **Consumer-Education and Homemaking Jobs** are:

1. Homemaker

2. Food-Processing Technician

3. Home Economist

4. Cook

Three more **Consumer-Education and Homemaking Jobs** are:

1. _____

2. _____

3. _____

In this booklet, Raul learns that running a home requires lots of jobs.

CAREER CRITTERS: CONSUMER-EDUCATION AND HOMEMAKING JOBS—STUDENT BOOKLET
© 1996 MAR∗CO PRODUCTS, INC. 1-800-448-2197

JOBS THAT HELP PEOPLE

Raul Raccoon was sweeping the floor. It was Saturday, and he was helping his mom and dad clean the house. "This is a lot of work," he said to his mom.

"That's right, Raul," answered Mom. "Homemaking is a big job, and it's a lot more than cleaning the house. It's everything you can think of that it takes to keep a home and family running smoothly."

CAREER CRITTERS: CONSUMER-EDUCATION AND HOMEMAKING JOBS—STUDENT BOOKLET
© 1996 MAR*CO PRODUCTS, INC. 1-800-448-2197

"There are lots of jobs that help make a home and family run smoothly. Selena Skunk's mom is a home economist," said Dad.

"A *what*?" asked Raul.

"A home economist," answered Dad. "She teaches people how to save money on food and clothing. She also teaches people to use things that will make their homes nicer. She works for the government. The government pays her to do this for families who need this kind of help."

4

"Bonnie Bear's mom also helps people," said Mom.

"How?" asked Raul. "Bonnie's mom works in a factory."

"That's right," said Mom. "She works in a food-processing factory. She inspects the food before it is put into stores to make sure it is safe to eat. Other people in her factory make sure the food is prepared and stored the right way. Without their jobs, people could buy food that might not be good to eat."

"Waldo Whale's uncle is a cook. But that doesn't count, because he doesn't cook at home," said Raul.

"In this case, it does," said Dad. "Waldo's uncle cooks on a ship in the Navy. When they're on the ship, the sailors are like a family. They work, sleep, and eat there. Waldo's uncle learned to cook after he joined the Navy. The Navy sent him to cooking school, and now he helps the sailors by cooking healthy meals for them."

"It sure takes a lot of jobs to make a family run smoothly," thought Raul. "And I guess sweeping is one of them."

HOMEMAKER MATH

Homemakers need to know math. Read the problems below. Write your answer in the square next each problem.

The light bulbs have burned out in the kitchen and garage. Each room has two light bulbs. How many bulbs will Dad have to buy to replace the burned-out light bulbs and have four extra bulbs on hand?

Mom wants her children to eat three kinds of fruit each day. She gave each child orange juice for breakfast, a banana for lunch, and an apple for a snack. How many more times do they need to eat fruit today?

It takes one gallon of paint to paint two rooms. Dad wants to paint the kitchen, living room, dining room, bathroom, and two bedrooms. How many gallons of paint should he buy?

CAREER CRITTERS: CONSUMER-EDUCATION AND HOMEMAKING JOBS—STUDENT BOOKLET
© 1996 MAR✳CO PRODUCTS, INC. 1-800-448-2197

Right now, I am _____ years old. This is a picture of me doing a **Consumer-Education and Homemaking Job**. Right now, this is what I think I might like to do.

BUT I CAN ALWAYS CHANGE MY MIND!

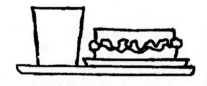

ENVIRONMENTAL CONTROL JOBS

ENVIRONMENTAL-CONTROL JOBS
LEADER'S GUIDE

If you are using puppets, select the bear, raccoon, Husky dog, and skunk.

Introduce the lesson by telling the students they will be learning about some jobs that help people and make their world a better place. They will also be learning a new word. Write *environment* on the chalkboard and explain that *environment* means the things that surround something. A bear's environment is the woods. Tell the students that *their* environment is the world around them.

Distribute the student booklets and pencils. Have the students complete the first page.

Have the students turn to the second page. Read the first part of the page with the students. When naming the four jobs listed on the page, tell the students that they will be learning about these jobs in their booklets.

Then ask the students to name some other jobs that involve environmental control. Write the appropriate answers on the chalkboard. Some examples could be: *park manager, urban planner, horticulturist, nursery worker, geologist, zoologist, botanist*. Have the students select three *Environmental-Control Jobs* and write them on the lines on the page. Read the last sentence on the page with the students.

Tell the students there will be several animal characters in the story and that some of the students will pretend to be the animal characters. (The skunk and Husky dog should be boys, and the raccoon and bear should be girls.) If you are using puppets, give each of the chosen students his/her puppet. Tell these students to sit near you during the lesson and that they will be involved in the story at certain times.

Have the students look at page 3. Read the text with the students. When you have finished reading, ask the following questions:

For the student holding the bear puppet:

- *Bonnie, would you like to be a forester? Why? Why not?*

For the rest of the students:

- *What would be the best thing about being a forester?*
- *What would be the hardest thing about being a forester?*

Have the students turn to page 4. Read the text with the students. When you have finished reading, ask the following questions:

For the student holding the skunk puppet:

- *Sidney, how does your aunt help everyone? (Everyone drinks water.)*
- *What would happen if water wasn't tested? (People and animals would get sick.)*

For the rest of the students:

- *Where does the water we drink come from? (lakes, rivers, and streams)*
- *After the water is tested, where does it go? (into homes and businesses)*
- *What happens to water no one drinks? (It returns to the plant through sewers, is purified, and sent to rivers and oceans.)*

Have the students look at page 5. Read the text with the students. When you have finished reading, ask the following questions:

For the student holding the raccoon puppet:

- *Rita, why is good soil important? (for healthy plants and animals)*

For the rest of the students:

- *If soil was poor and plants were not healthy, what would happen to our food supply? (Less food would be produced.)*

Have the students turn to page 6. Read the text with the students. When you have finished reading, ask the following questions:

For the student holding the Husky dog puppet:

- *Hanuk, why do you think your grandfather's job could be dangerous? (He might run into people who didn't care if they broke the law. He would have to arrest them when they hurt or killed animals.)*

For the rest of the students:

- *How do you think people who work in environmental-control jobs feel about their work?*

For the student holding the bear puppet:

- *Bonnie, what do you think would happen to the trees if there were no foresters?*

For the student holding the skunk puppet:

- *Sidney, what do think would happen to the water if there were no water-treatment plant operators?*

For the student holding the raccoon puppet:

- *Rita, what would happen if there were no soil scientists?*

For the student holding the Husky dog puppet:

- *Hanuk, what do you think would happen to the animals if there were no game wardens?*

For the rest of the students:

- *Do you think there will be a need for environmental-control workers when you grow up? Why? Why not?*

If puppets were used in the lesson, collect them from the students.

Give the students crayons or markers and have them complete the activities on pages 7 and 8. If they finish before the allotted time has elapsed, tell them they may color the pictures on other pages.

Conclude the lesson by asking the students why they believe *Environmental-Control Jobs* are important. Tell the students they may take their booklets home to share with their parents.

ENVIRONMENTAL-CONTROL JOBS

NAME

TEACHER

GRADE

1

The world around us—our plants, animals, water, air, and soil—is our *environment*. Our environment needs help so it is not harmed. Many people work in jobs to make that happen. Their jobs are called **Environmental-Control Jobs.**

Four **Environmental-Control Jobs** are:

1. Forester

2. Game Warden

3. Water-Treatment Plant Operator

4. Soil Scientist

Three more **Environmental-Control Jobs** are:

1. _____

2. _____

3. _____

This booklet is about jobs that help protect our forests, water, animals, and soil.

CAREER CRITTERS: ENVIRONMENTAL-CONTROL JOBS—STUDENT BOOKLET
© 1996 MAR*CO PRODUCTS, INC. 1-800-448-2197

PROTECTING SOIL, WATER, AND ANIMALS

Bonnie Bear was sitting at her desk in Animaltown Elementary School. The teacher was telling the class how important it is to protect trees, water, and animals. Bonnie raised her hand and said, "My dad is a forester. He protects trees. He tells the lumber company what trees to cut and when to plant new ones. He's helping the environment." The teacher agreed, and Bonnie felt very proud.

3

Sidney Skunk told about his aunt working in the water-treatment plant. She makes sure water is safe to drink. That helps the environment, too.

CAREER CRITTERS: ENVIRONMENTAL-CONTROL JOBS—STUDENT BOOKLET
© 1996 MAR∗CO PRODUCTS, INC. 1-800-448-2197

Rita Raccoon told about her dad, a soil scientist. Farmers come to him to learn what crops will grow best in their soil and how to make their soil better.

CAREER CRITTERS: ENVIRONMENTAL-CONTROL JOBS—STUDENT BOOKLET
© 1996 MAR✳CO PRODUCTS, INC. 1-800-448-2197

Before the recess bell rang, Hanuk Husky told the class about his grandfather, who is a game warden. His grandfather makes sure people don't kill animals when they shouldn't. He checks to see that the animals are not sick or hurt.

Bonnie never knew so many jobs helped protect her environment. She felt her world really was a safer place because of these workers and their jobs.

CAREER CRITTERS: ENVIRONMENTAL-CONTROL JOBS—STUDENT BOOKLET
© 1996 MAR*CO PRODUCTS, INC. 1-800-448-2197

DOT-TO-DOT

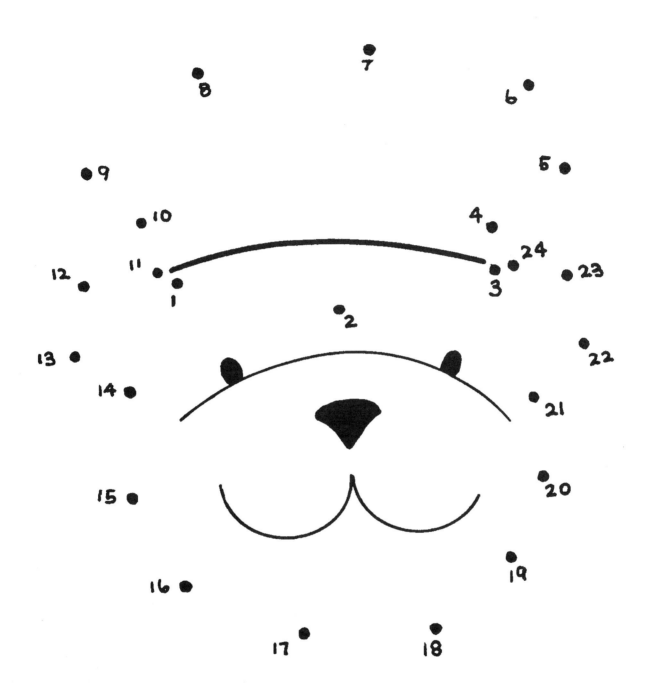

This is Bonnie Bear's uncle. He is a park ranger. It is his job to see that people obey the rules in the park. He also protects the animals and plants in the park.

CAREER CRITTERS: ENVIRONMENTAL-CONTROL JOBS—STUDENT BOOKLET
© 1996 MAR✳CO PRODUCTS, INC. 1-800-448-2197

Right now, I am _____ years old. This is a picture of me doing an **Environmental-Control Job**. Right now, this is what I think I might like to do.

BUT I CAN ALWAYS CHANGE MY MIND!

CAREER CRITTERS: ENVIRONMENTAL-CONTROL JOBS—STUDENT BOOKLET
© 1996 MAR*CO PRODUCTS, INC. 1-800-448-2197

FINE ARTS
AND
HUMANITIES
JOBS

FINE ARTS AND HUMANITIES JOBS
LEADER'S GUIDE

If you are using puppets, select the donkey, squirrel, bear, and whale.

Introduce the lesson by telling the students they will be learning about some jobs that they see on television, in the movies, and in museums.

Distribute the student booklets and pencils. Have the students complete the first page. Tell the students that people who make their living acting in television or the movies, painting pictures, designing clothes, playing music, translating languages, and interpreting religions are said to have jobs in *Fine Arts and Humanities*.

Have the students turn to the second page. Read the first part of the page with the students. When naming the four jobs listed on the page, have the students tell where they might see people doing these jobs.

Then ask the students to name some other jobs that involve *Fine Arts and Humanities*. Write the appropriate answers on the chalkboard. Some examples could be: *commercial artist, composer, poet, interior designer, jewelry maker, film editor, interpreter, make-up artist, writer, minister/priest/rabbi, sculptor*. Have the students select three *Fine Arts and Humanities Jobs* and write them on the lines on the page. Read the last sentence on the page with the students.

Tell the students there will be several animal characters in the story and that some of the students will pretend to be the animal characters. (The squirrel and donkey should be boys, and the bear and whale should be girls.) If you are using puppets, give each of the chosen students his/her puppet. Tell these students to sit near you during the lesson and that they will be involved in the story at certain times.

Have the students look at page 3. Read the text with the students. When you have finished reading, ask the following questions:

For the student holding the donkey puppet:

- *Danny, how did you feel when you heard your voice?*
- *How did your feelings change when Sammy told you to play your drums?*

For the student holding the squirrel puppet:

- *Sammy, why did you decide to tell Danny about playing the drums?*

For the rest of the students:

- *How many different jobs can you name that have to do with music?*
- *What would be the hardest thing about being a musician?*
- *What would be the best thing about being a musician?*

Have the students turn to page 4. Read the text with the students. When you have finished reading, ask the following questions:

For the student holding the bear puppet:

- *Bonnie, what happened to make you change your mind about dancing? (Sammy told her she was a good dancer.)*

For the student holding the squirrel puppet:

- *Sammy, why did you decide to tell Bonnie how you felt about her dancing?*

For the rest of the students:

- *How many jobs can you name that have to do with dancing?*
- *What would be the hardest thing about being a dancer?*
- *What would be the best thing about being a dancer?*

Have the students look at page 5. Read the text with the students. When you have finished reading, ask the following questions:

For the student holding the whale puppet:

- *Winnie, why do you think you were afraid to get up in front of people? (She was afraid she would be embarrassed.)*

CAREER CRITTERS © MAR✻CO PRODUCTS, INC. 1-800-448-2197

For the student holding the squirrel puppet:

- *Sammy, why did you decide to help Winnie?*

For the rest of the students:

- *How many jobs can you name that have to do with singing?*
- *What would be the hardest thing about being a singer?*
- *What would be the best thing about being a singer?*

Have the students turn to page 6. Read the text with the students. When you have finished reading, ask the following questions:

For the student holding the squirrel puppet:

- *Sammy, how did you feel when your friends helped you?*

For the rest of the students:

- *How many jobs can you name that have to do with art?*
- *What would be the hardest thing about being an artist?*
- *What would be the best thing about being an artist?*

If puppets were used in the lesson, collect them from the students.

Give the students crayons or markers and have them complete the activities on pages 7 and 8. If they finish before the allotted time has elapsed, tell them they may color the pictures on other pages.

Conclude the lesson by having the students share their activity pages with the class. Then tell the students they may take their booklets home to share with their parents.

FINE ARTS
AND
HUMANITIES JOBS

NAME

TEACHER

GRADE

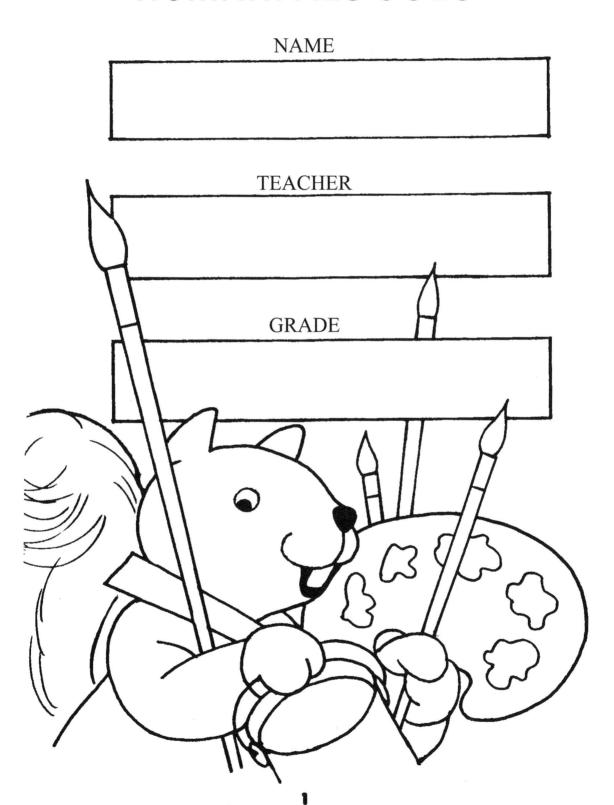

1

Did you ever see a dancer on television? Did you ever see a picture of someone making fancy clothes? Did you ever watch someone paint a picture? All of these people have **Fine Arts and Humanities Jobs**. They earn money for dancing on the stage, designing clothes, and painting pictures. Some people say people who do these things have special talents.

Four **Fine Arts and Humanities Jobs** are:

1. Singer

2. Musician

3. Dancer

4. Artist

Three more **Fine Arts and Humanities Jobs** are:

1. _____

2. _____

3. _____

In this booklet, Sammy learns talent has many different forms.

CAREER CRITTERS: FINE ARTS AND HUMANITIES JOBS—STUDENT BOOKLET
© 1996 MAR✳CO PRODUCTS, INC. 1-800-448-2197

SAMMY'S TALENT

Danny Donkey let out a loud "Hee haw!" Everyone covered their ears. "Singing for the talent show is not a good idea," said Danny. "I'm just not musical."

"What are you saying?" asked Sammy Squirrel. "I know you play the drums. My uncle plays drums. He's a grown-up and he gets paid for playing in a band. Who knows? Maybe some day you will be playing your drums on a stage."

Danny thought, "It's possible." And off he went to get his drums.

CAREER CRITTERS: FINE ARTS AND HUMANITIES JOBS—STUDENT BOOKLET
© 1996 MAR✳CO PRODUCTS, INC. 1-800-448-2197

Sammy saw Bonnie Bear standing on her toes and twirling. When he went over to tell her how good she was, he saw a sour look on her face. "What's wrong, Bonnie?" he asked.

"I hate this dancing. My mom makes me take the lessons."

"But you're so good!" Sammy said. "I bet you could be a ballerina some day." Bonnie's face lit up.

When the teacher called Bonnie's name, she went onto the stage smiling. "Someone thinks I'm good," she thought to herself.

CAREER CRITTERS: FINE ARTS AND HUMANITIES JOBS—STUDENT BOOKLET
© 1996 MAR✳CO PRODUCTS, INC. 1-800-448-2197

Winnie Whale was sitting alone in the corner. "What's the matter?" asked Sammy.

"I'm scared. I hate getting up in front of people. I'm afraid I'll open my mouth and nothing will come out."

"Don't look at them. Look over their heads," said Sammy. "Try it, you'll be surprised." A few minutes later, Sammy heard a beautiful voice. It was Winnie! She was looking right over the teacher's head. Sammy thought that with a voice like that, Winnie might be an opera star some day.

CAREER CRITTERS: FINE ARTS AND HUMANITIES JOBS—STUDENT BOOKLET
© 1996 MAR∗CO PRODUCTS, INC. 1-800-448-2197

The talent show was a big event. All of Sammy Squirrel's friends were in it. Sammy had helped them all, but he could not help himself. He felt left out. Danny, Bonnie, and Winnie were worried about Sammy. He looked very sad as he sat drawing at his desk. The three friends thought and thought. Then Winnie said, "Why can't Sammy make the invitations and the scenery?" It was a great idea, and Sammy learned that not all talent belongs on a stage. Some of it hangs on walls, like the scenery he made for the talent show.

CAREER CRITTERS: FINE ARTS AND HUMANITIES JOBS—STUDENT BOOKLET
© 1996 MAR✳CO PRODUCTS, INC. 1-800-448-2197

I MIGHT LIKE TO BE...

Below are pictures of people who have **Fine Arts and Humanities Jobs.** Circle all the pictures that show something you think you might like to do. Then count the number of pictures you have circled and write that number on the line at the bottom of this page.

I have circled _____ pictures on this page.

CAREER CRITTERS: FINE ARTS AND HUMANITIES JOBS—STUDENT BOOKLET
© 1996 MAR✱CO PRODUCTS, INC. 1-800-448-2197

Right now, I am _____ years old. This is a picture of me doing a **Fine Arts and Humanities Job**. Right now, this is what I think I might like to do.

BUT I CAN ALWAYS CHANGE MY MIND!

CAREER CRITTERS: FINE ARTS AND HUMANITIES JOBS—STUDENT BOOKLET
© 1996 MAR✳CO PRODUCTS, INC. 1-800-448-2197

HEALTHCARE JOBS

HEALTHCARE JOBS
LEADER'S GUIDE

If you are using puppets, select the donkey, raccoon, Husky dog, and squirrel.

Introduce the lesson by telling the students they will be learning about some jobs that help make people well and keep them healthy. They are called *Healthcare Jobs.*

Distribute the student booklets and pencils. Have the students complete the first page.

Have the students turn to the second page. Read the first part of the page with the students. When naming the four jobs listed on the page, tell the students that they will be learning about these jobs in their booklets.

Then ask the students to name some other jobs that involve *Healthcare.* Write the appropriate answers on the chalkboard. Some examples could be: *chiropractor, dental hygienist, nurse's aide, obstetrician, optometrist, pediatrician, physical therapist, psychiatrist, x-ray technician.* Have the students select three *Healthcare Jobs* and write them on the lines on the page. Read the last sentences on the page with the students.

Tell the students there will be several animal characters in the story and that some of the students will pretend to be the animal characters. (The squirrel and donkey should be boys, and the raccoon and Husky dog should be girls.) If you are using puppets, give each of the chosen students his/her puppet. Tell these students to sit near you during the lesson and that they will be involved in the story at certain times.

Have the students look at page 3. Read the text with the students. When you have finished reading, ask the following questions:

For the student holding the raccoon puppet:

• *Rita, why were you so excited about your grandfather coming to school?*

For the rest of the students:

• *If your class was studying about Healthcare Jobs, who would you bring to class?*

Have the students turn to page 4. Read the text with the students. When you have finished reading, ask the following questions:

For the student holding the raccoon puppet:

- *Rita, what were some of the things your grandfather showed the class? (instruments or other things doctors might use)*

For the rest of the students:

- *Rita's grandfather helps children. What is this kind of doctor called? (a pediatrician)*

- *What other kinds of doctors can you name? (Accept any correct answers.)*

For the student holding the donkey puppet:

- *Danny, why do you think the dentist says brushing teeth is important? (To prevent cavities, keep teeth clean, etc.)*

For the rest of the students:

- *What are some things dentists do besides tell people to brush their teeth? (pull teeth, fill cavities, etc.)*

Have the students look at page 5. Read the text with the students. When you have finished reading, ask the following questions:

For the student holding the Husky dog puppet:

- *Hanna, why would knowing how to measure correctly be important for a pharmacist? (to be able to measure the correct amounts of medicine)*

For the rest of the students:

- *Where besides a drug store might a pharmacist work? (in a hospital, clinic, etc.)*

CAREER CRITTERS © MAR✳CO PRODUCTS, INC. 1-800-448-2197

For the student holding the squirrel puppet:

- *Sammy, how does your uncle help the doctors in the hospital? (gives medicine the doctors prescribe, assists in the operating room, etc.)*

For the rest of the class:

- *Where besides hospitals do nurses work? (doctors' offices, clinics, schools, businesses, etc.)*

Have the students turn to page 6. Read the text with the students. When you have finished reading, ask the following questions:

For the student holding the raccoon puppet:

- *Rita, why were you proud of your grandfather?*

For the rest of the students:

- *Why do you think you have to go to college for most Healthcare Jobs? (It takes a lot of time and special schooling to learn about the body.)*
- *Can you think of any Healthcare Jobs for which a person would not need to go to college? (nurse's aide, medical secretary, although these jobs do require special training.)*

If puppets were used in the lesson, collect them from the students.

Give the students crayons or markers and have them complete the activities on pages 7 and 8. If they finish before the allotted time has elapsed, tell them they may color the pictures on other pages. When the students have finished, discuss page 7 and how veterinarians are also a part of the healthcare field because they help make sick animals well.

Conclude the lesson by having the students share their activity pages with the class. Then tell the students they may take their booklets home to share with their parents.

HEALTHCARE JOBS

NAME

TEACHER

GRADE

1

Many people help us when we are sick. These people work at **Healthcare Jobs.** Healthcare workers work in many different places. Some work in hospitals. Others work in offices or clinics. Still others work in businesses and schools.

Four **Healthcare Jobs** are:

1. Doctor

2. Dentist

3. Pharmacist

4. Nurse

Three more **Healthcare Jobs** are:

1. _____

2. _____

3. _____

Rita Raccoon's class will learn about **Healthcare Jobs** today, when lots of people come to visit. That is what this booklet is all about.

HELPING PEOPLE
STAY HEALTHY

Rita Raccoon can hardly wait to go to school! Her class is studying about careers, and today is the day for them to learn about jobs in healthcare. That means Rita's grandfather is coming to talk to her class. He is a doctor, and he is going to walk to school with her today.

Rita's grandfather told the children that he works in a clinic, where he helps children get well. He showed the class some of the things he uses when someone is sick. Then he told them that to be a doctor, he needed to study hard in school and go to college for a long time.

Then Danny Donkey introduced his neighbor. She is a dentist. She told the class how important it is for people to take care of their teeth. She showed the students how to brush their teeth properly, and gave everyone a toothbrush.

CAREER CRITTERS: HEALTHCARE JOBS—STUDENT BOOKLET
© 1996 MAR✱CO PRODUCTS, INC. 1-800-448-2197

Hanna Husky introduced her friend, who works at the drug store. He is a pharmacist. He fills the prescriptions doctors order for their patients. A pharmacist must be very careful and be sure people get the right medicine.

The last speaker was Sammy Squirrel's uncle. He is a nurse. He works with the doctors in the hospital. He did not have to go to school as long as the doctors, but he *did* have to go to college. He said the best part of his job is seeing patients go home after they get well.

Rita Raccoon was very excited when she came home. She had a lot to tell her mother. She told her how proud she was of her grandfather. She also told her that for most jobs that have to do with helping people stay healthy, you have to study hard and go to college.

CAREER CRITTERS: HEALTHCARE JOBS—STUDENT BOOKLET
© 1996 MAR∗CO PRODUCTS, INC. 1-800-448-2197

DOT-TO-DOT

This dog is sick. Follow the dots to see who will help him. When you finish, you will have a picture of a veterinarian.

CAREER CRITTERS: HEALTHCARE JOBS—STUDENT BOOKLET
© 1996 MAR✶CO PRODUCTS, INC. 1-800-448-2197

Right now, I am _____ years old. This is a picture of me doing a **Healthcare Job.** Right now, this is what I think I might like to do.

BUT I CAN ALWAYS CHANGE MY MIND!

CAREER CRITTERS: HEALTHCARE JOBS—STUDENT BOOKLET
© 1996 MAR∗CO PRODUCTS, INC. 1-800-448-2197

HOSPITALITY AND RECREATION JOBS

HOSPITALITY AND RECREATION JOBS
LEADER'S GUIDE

If you are using puppets, select the donkey, squirrel, skunk, and whale.

Introduce the lesson by telling the students they will be learning about some jobs that help people relax and have fun.

Distribute the student booklets and pencils. Have the students complete the first page. Tell the students that people who make a living arranging vacations, working on airplanes, working in hotels, and working in parks are said to have jobs in *Hospitality and Recreation*. Explain that *hospitality* means welcoming and being nice to guests and *recreation* means fun or relaxing activities.

Have the students turn to the second page. Read the first part of the page with the students. When naming the four jobs listed on the page, have the students tell how each might help people relax and have fun.

Then ask the students to name some other jobs that involve *Hospitality and Recreation*. Write the appropriate answers on the chalkboard. Some examples could be: *Camp Counselor, Comedian, Athlete, Acrobat, Magician.* Have the students select three *Hospitality and Recreation Jobs* and write them on the lines on the page. Read the last sentences on the page with the students.

Tell the students there will be several animal characters in the story and that some of the students will pretend to be the animal characters. (The skunk and whale should be boys, and the squirrel and donkey should be girls.) If you are using puppets, give each of the chosen students his/her puppet. Tell these students to sit near you during the lesson and that they will be involved in the story at certain times.

Have the students look at page 3. Read the text with the students. When you have finished reading, ask the following questions:

For the student holding the squirrel puppet:

- *Shanna, how did you feel when you heard you were going on a airplane to take a vacation?*

For the student holding the skunk puppet:

- *Sidney, if you could have your grandfather plan a vacation anywhere in the world for you and your family, where would it be?*

For the rest of the students:

- *How many different jobs can you name that have something to do with vacations?*
- *What would be the hardest thing about being a travel agent?*
- *What would be the best thing about being a travel agent?*

Have the students turn to page 4. Read the text with the students. When you have finished reading, ask the following questions:

For the student holding the donkey puppet:

- *Doree, what is it like to have a mother who is a flight attendant?*

For the rest of the students:

- *How many jobs can you name that have to do with airplanes?*
- *What would be the hardest thing about being a flight attendant?*
- *What would be the best thing about being a flight attendant?*

Have the students look at page 5. Read the text with the students. When you have finished reading, ask the following questions:

For the student holding the squirrel puppet:

- *Shanna, what would be the best thing about staying in a hotel?*

For the student holding the whale puppet:

- *Waldo, what is the best thing about having an aunt who works at a hotel?*

For the rest of the students:

- *How many jobs can you name that have to do with hotels?*
- *What would be the hardest thing about working in a hotel?*
- *What would be the best thing about working in a hotel?*

Have the students turn to page 6. Read the text with the students. When you have finished reading, ask the following questions:

For the student holding the whale puppet:

- *Waldo, what do you think the people playing water games thought of your aunt?*

For the rest of the students:

- *How many jobs can you name that have to do with swimming pools?*
- *What would be the hardest thing about being an activities director?*
- *What would be the best thing about being an activities director?*

If puppets were used in the lesson, collect them from the students.

Give the students crayons or markers and have them complete the activities on pages 7 and 8. If they finish before the allotted time has elapsed, tell them they may color the pictures on other pages.

Conclude the lesson by having the students share their activity pages with the class. Then tell the students they may take their booklets home to share with their parents.

HOSPITALITY AND RECREATION JOBS

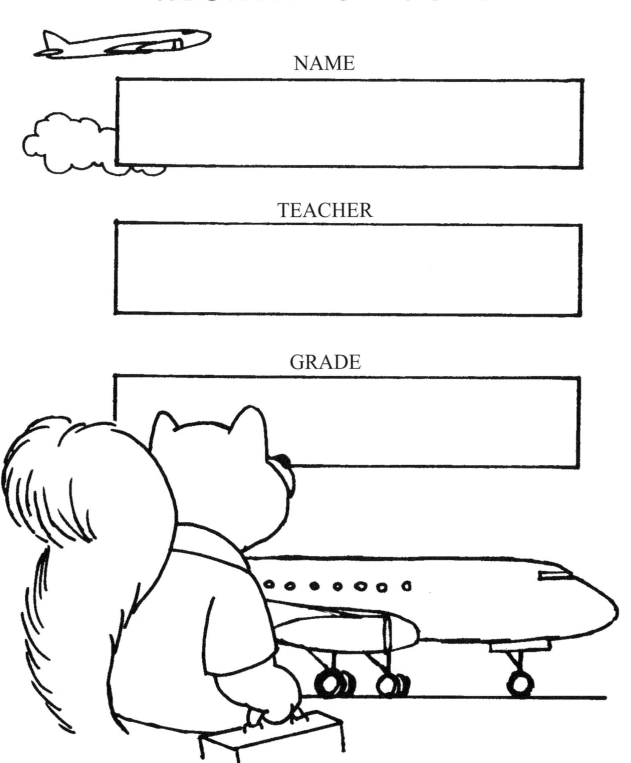

NAME

TEACHER

GRADE

1

People like to relax and have fun. They do this by going on vacations, having hobbies, or doing things they enjoy around the house. There are many jobs that have to do with helping people relax and have fun. These are jobs in **Hospitality and Recreation.**

Four **Hospitality and Recreation Jobs** are:

1. Travel Agent

2. Hotel Clerk

3. Flight Attendant

4. Activities Director

Three more **Hospitality and Recreation Jobs** are:

1. _____

2. _____

3. _____

In this booklet, a squirrel named Shanna goes on a vacation. She discovers that people doing many different jobs help her have fun.

CAREER CRITTERS: HOSPITALITY AND RECREATION JOBS—STUDENT BOOKLET
© 1996 MAR*CO PRODUCTS, INC. 1-800-448-2197

VACATION AND FUN

Shanna Squirrel is going on a vacation. Her parents decided to go to Sidney Skunk's grandfather's travel agency to plan their trip. At the travel agency, Sidney's grandfather helped them choose one of many different vacations. They decided to fly to another state, where they would stay in a fancy hotel near a national park. Shanna and her parents were happy. Sidney's grandfather was happy he had helped them.

CAREER CRITTERS: HOSPITALITY AND RECREATION JOBS—STUDENT BOOKLET
© 1996 MAR✶CO PRODUCTS, INC. 1-800-448-2197

On the day of her trip, Shanna went to the airport and boarded the airplane. She was greeted by a flight attendant, Ms. Donkey, who said she had a daughter named Doree.

During the flight, Ms. Donkey brought Shanna drinks, snacks, and even a blanket and pillow. Shanna felt her vacation was off to a wonderful start, and Ms. Donkey was happy to be a part of making Shanna feel good.

CAREER CRITTERS: HOSPITALITY AND RECREATION JOBS—STUDENT BOOKLET
© 1996 MAR✳CO PRODUCTS, INC. 1-800-448-2197

When Shanna reached the hotel, her family was well taken care of. A hotel clerk checked them in, a porter carried their bags, and Room Service delivered their meals right to the room. Shanna thought that this was the greatest vacation ever. At the hotel, Shanna met a new friend, Waldo Whale. Waldo said his aunt was the director of water activities. Shanna could hardly wait to meet her.

CAREER CRITTERS: HOSPITALITY AND RECREATION JOBS—STUDENT BOOKLET
© 1996 MAR∗CO PRODUCTS, INC. 1-800-448-2197

All during her vacation, Shanna joined in many water activities. Waldo was always there, and his aunt would explain the rules and teach everyone how to play the games. Everybody had fun, especially Shanna. She was having the best vacation, and Waldo Whale was happy to be sharing Shanna's good time. Shanna wished her vacation would never end. But when it did, Shanna had many great memories.

CAREER CRITTERS: HOSPITALITY AND RECREATION JOBS—STUDENT BOOKLET
© 1996 MAR✴CO PRODUCTS, INC. 1-800-448-2197

WHAT I MIGHT LIKE TO BE

Circle the pictures that show what you might like to be.

Right now, I am _____ years old. This is a picture of me doing a **Hospitality and Recreation Job.** Right now, this is what I think I might like to do.

BUT I CAN ALWAYS CHANGE MY MIND!

CAREER CRITTERS: HOSPITALITY AND RECREATION JOBS—STUDENT BOOKLET
© 1996 MAR*CO PRODUCTS, INC. 1-800-448-2197

MANUFACTURING JOBS

MANUFACTURING JOBS
LEADER'S GUIDE

If you are using puppets, select the donkey, raccoon, Husky dog, and skunk.

Introduce the lesson by telling the students they will be learning about some jobs that help people have things that will make their lives better. They will also be learning a new word. Write the word *manufacturing* on the chalkboard. Tell the students this word means something that is made by hand or machine. Things that are *manufactured* make our lives better.

Distribute the student booklets and pencils. Have the students complete the first page.

Have the students turn to the second page. Read the first part of the page with the students. When naming the four jobs listed on the page, tell the students that they will be learning about these jobs in their booklets.

Then ask the students to name some other jobs that involve *Manufacturing*. Write the appropriate answers on the chalkboard. Some examples could be: *electrical engineer, chemist, printer, sheet metal worker, welder.* Have the students select three *Manufacturing Jobs* and write them on the lines on the page. Read the last sentences on the page with the students.

Tell the students there will be several animal characters in the story and that some of the students will pretend to be the animal characters. (The raccoon and Husky dog should be boys, and the donkey and skunk should be girls.) If you are using puppets, give each of the chosen students his/her puppet. Tell these students to sit near you during the lesson and that they will be involved in the story at certain times.

Have the students look at page 3. Read the text with the students. When you have finished reading, ask the following questions:

For the student holding the donkey puppet:

- *Doree, if you had money, could you go into a department store and not buy anything? Why? Why not?*

For the rest of the students:

- *How many jobs can you name that have to do with shopping?*

Have the students turn to page 4. Read the text with the students. When you have finished reading, ask the following questions:

For the student holding the Husky dog puppet:

- *Hanuk, what is your favorite toy? Would it be made in your aunt's factory?*
- *How would you feel if you could make toys?*

For the rest of the students:

- *How many jobs can you name that have to do with toys?*
- *What would be the hardest thing about being a toy maker?*
- *What would be the best thing about being a toy maker?*

Have the students turn to page 5. Read the text with the students. When you have finished reading, ask the following questions:

For the student holding the raccoon puppet:

- *Raul, what kinds of clothing do you think your uncle makes?*

For the rest of the students:

- *How many jobs can you name that have to do with clothes?*
- *What would be the hardest thing about being a tailor?*
- *What would be the best thing about being a tailor?*

Have the students turn to page 6. Read the text with the students. When you have finished reading, ask the following questions:

For the student holding the skunk puppet:

- *Selena, what kinds of furniture does your grandfather upholster?*
- *Why would your grandfather have to know about measuring? (so he could cut material the correct size to fit the chairs or sofas)*

CAREER CRITTERS © MAR✳CO PRODUCTS, INC. 1-800-448-2197

For the rest of the students:

- *How many jobs can you name that have to do with furniture?*
- *What is the hardest thing about being an upholsterer?*
- *What is the best thing about being an upholsterer?*

If puppets were used in the lesson, collect them from the students.

Give the students crayons or markers and have them complete the activities on pages 7 and 8. If they finish before the allotted time has elapsed, tell them they may color the pictures on other pages.

Conclude the lesson by asking the students to tell you why they believe *Manufacturing Jobs* are important. Then tell the students they may take their booklets home to share with their parents.

MANUFACTURING JOBS

NAME

TEACHER

GRADE

People buy things from stores every day. Do you ever wonder where all these things come from? They come from factories that make products for stores to sell. There are many jobs that have to do with making the products we buy. These are jobs in **Manufacturing**.

Four **Manufacturing Jobs** are:

1. Assembler

2. Tailor

3. Sewing Machine Operator

4. Upholsterer

Three more **Manufacturing Jobs** are:

1. _____

2. _____

3. _____

In this booklet, a donkey named Doree goes shopping. In the store, she discovers that it takes many different workers to make all the things that are for sale.

DOREE GOES SHOPPING

Doree Donkey is going shopping. She loves to shop. Even if she doesn't buy anything, she loves to look at all the different things for sale. Today, Doree is going to a big department store. This store sells just about everything. Doree has never been to a store this big before, and she is really looking forward to it. Now that she is ready, off to the store she goes!

CAREER CRITTERS: MANUFACTURING JOBS—STUDENT BOOKLET
© 1996 MAR✳CO PRODUCTS, INC. 1-800-448-2197

In the store, Doree goes to the toy department. A salesperson says, "Hi! May I help you?"

Doree says, "Yes, show me everything." So the salesperson shows Doree all the different toys. Doree can't believe all the toys! She asks, "Where is the room where you make all these toys?"

The salesperson answers, "We don't make toys here. They are made by toy assemblers in a toy factory. Hanuk Husky's aunt works there."

Then Doree goes to the clothing department. The salesperson shows her pants, shirts, socks, and hats. Doree is amazed at all the different kinds of clothes. She asks, "Can I see the room where you make all these clothes?"

The salesperson answers, "We don't make the clothes here. They're made in a big clothing factory by tailors and sewing machine operators like Raul Raccoon's uncle and aunt."

CAREER CRITTERS: MANUFACTURING JOBS—STUDENT BOOKLET
© 1996 MAR✳CO PRODUCTS, INC. 1-800-448-2197

Doree Donkey sees the store manager talking with a salesperson. As Doree approaches them, she says, "Hi! Do you work here?"

The salesperson replies, "No. I work for a furniture manufacturer. Our factory makes the best couches and chairs, made by the best upholsterers, like Selena's Skunk's grandfather." Upholsterers cover furniture with fabric they have measured and cut.

"We're going to sell that furniture in this store," says the manager.

Doree thought how glad she was that she had gone to the store and asked questions. Now she really *does* understand manufacturing.

WHAT WOULD YOU MAKE?

Draw a picture of something you would like to make that could be sold in a store.

Right now, I am _____ years old. This is a picture of me doing a **Manufacturing Job.** Right now, this is what I think I might like to do.

BUT I CAN ALWAYS CHANGE MY MIND!

CAREER CRITTERS: MANUFACTURING JOBS—STUDENT BOOKLET

MARINE SCIENCE JOBS

MARINE SCIENCE JOBS
LEADER'S GUIDE

If you are using puppets, select the bear, raccoon, whale, and donkey.

Introduce the lesson by telling the students they will be learning about some jobs that have to do with water and the animals and plants that live in water. They will also be learning a new word. Write the word *marine* on the chalkboard. Tell the students that this word refers to the sea. *Marine Science Jobs* have to do with learning about the sea and making it healthier.

Distribute the student booklets and pencils. Have the students complete the first page.

Have the students turn to the second page. Read the first part of the page with the students. When naming the four jobs listed on the page, tell the students that they will be learning about these jobs in their booklets.

Then ask the students to name some other jobs that involve *Marine Science*. Write the appropriate answers on the chalkboard. Some examples could be: *aquanaut* (study undersea life), *deep-sea diver* (walk on the bottom of the ocean to study and bring up things from the ocean floor), *fish hatcher* (raise fish until they are ready to be put into oceans or lakes), *ocean mapper* (make maps of the ocean floor). If necessary, explain each job by using the brief definition in parentheses. Have the students select three *Marine Science Jobs* and write them on the lines on the page. Read the last sentences on the page with the students.

Tell the students there will be several animal characters in the story and that some of the students will pretend to be the animal characters. (The whale and bear should be boys, and the raccoon and donkey should be girls.) If you are using puppets, give each of the chosen students his/her puppet. Tell these students to sit near you during the lesson and that they will be involved in the story at certain times.

Have the students look at page 3. Read the text with the students. When you have finished reading, ask the following questions:

For the student holding the whale puppet:

* *Waldo, how did you feel when the kids laughed at you?*

For the rest of the students:

- *Why do you think the kids did not take Waldo seriously when he said they should not waste water?*
- *What is it called when chemicals are dumped into the water and hurt fish and other sea life? (pollution)*

Have the students turn to page 4. Read the text with the students. When you have finished reading, ask the following questions:

For the student holding the donkey puppet:

- *Doree, what job in the aquarium would you like best?*

For the rest of the students:

- *What are some jobs an aquarist might do? (clean fish tanks, feed fish, transfer fish from one tank to another, etc.)*

Have the students look at page 5. Read the text with the students. When you have finished reading, ask the following questions:

For the student holding the raccoon puppet:

- *Rita, would being a hydrologist be a good job for a person who did not like to be outdoors? Why or why not?*

For the rest of the students:

- *What do you think might be in the water that the hydrologist would want to know about? (poisonous metals, bacteria, sewage, etc.)*

Have the students turn to page 6. Read the text with the students. When you have finished reading, ask the following questions:

For the student holding the bear puppet:

- *Bono, why would a marine biologist have to be very careful? (Not being accurate might destroy or contaminate samples.)*

For the rest of the students:

- *What kinds of books do you think a marine biologist might have been interested in at your age?*
- *Why do you think the boys and girls stopped laughing at Waldo?*

If puppets were used in the lesson, collect them from the students.

Give the students crayons or markers and have them complete the activities on pages 7 and 8. If they finish before the allotted time has elapsed, tell them they may color the pictures on other pages.

Conclude the lesson by having the students share their activity pages with the class. Then tell the students they may take their booklets home to share with their parents.

MARINE SCIENCE JOBS

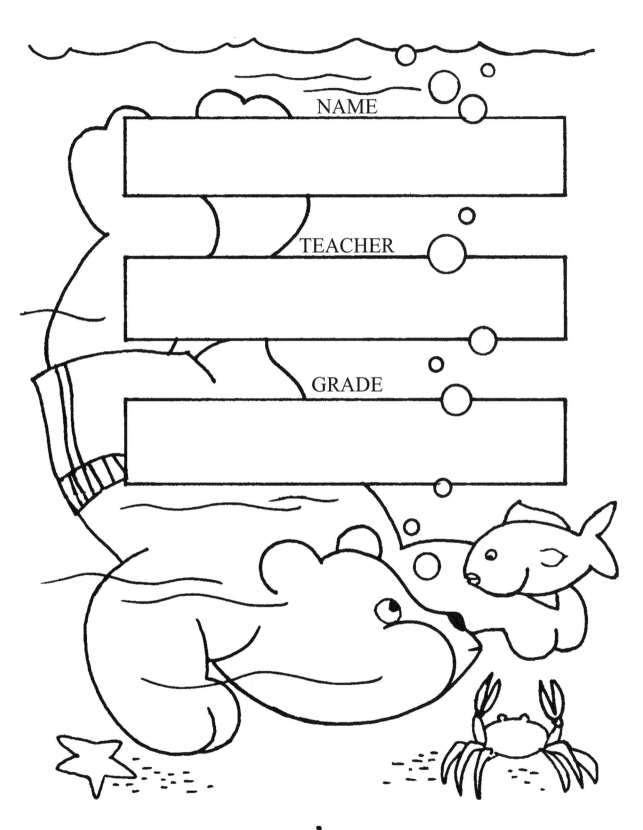

NAME

TEACHER

GRADE

1

Water is important to the life of animals and plants. The word *marine* means having to do with the sea. People who work in jobs that help them learn about water and its plants and animals have **Marine Science Jobs**. Some of these jobs have very long names.

Four **Marine Science Jobs** are:

1. Marine Biologist

2. Hydrologist

3. Oceanographer

4. Aquarist

Three more **Marine Science Jobs** are:

1. _____

2. _____

3. _____

In this booklet, Waldo Whale's class takes a field trip to an aquarium. This booklet is about jobs that have to do with water.

WATER IS SERIOUS BUSINESS

Waldo Whale's class was taking a field trip to the aquarium. It was going to be a great day. Sometimes, the kids laughed at Waldo when he tried to tell them how important it was not to waste water. His grandmother had told him that, and she is an oceanographer. She studies the ocean to learn how deep it is and what chemicals are in it. She hates some of the chemicals being dumped into the ocean, because they hurt the fish and other sea life.

CAREER CRITTERS: MARINE SCIENCE JOBS—STUDENT BOOKLET
© 1996 MAR∗CO PRODUCTS, INC. 1-800-448-2197

When the class arrived at the aquarium, the aquarist met them. Doree Donkey had a secret smile on her face. The aquarist was her neighbor. He told the class that it is his job to make sure that the fish and plants have a good, healthy life at the aquarium. He told them that he does a lot of things. He even cuts up the food for the fish.

4

After the field trip, the class began discussing jobs that have to do with water. Rita Raccoon said she knew a lady whose main job is to study water. She takes samples of water from rivers and lakes to learn about what is in it.

She also studies underground water called *springs* and makes maps of them. She is called a hydrologist, because *hydro* means water in another language.

CAREER CRITTERS: MARINE SCIENCE JOBS—STUDENT BOOKLET
© 1996 MAR∗CO PRODUCTS, INC. 1-800-448-2197

Bono Bear spoke up next. He has an uncle who lives far away and studies all about the plants and animals in the water. He is a marine biologist. Bono told the class that anyone who wants to do the kind of work his uncle does must study hard and go to college.

Waldo looked around the room. No one was laughing. They knew now that what he had said about water was true, and they never laughed at him again.

WHAT DO MARINE SCIENTISTS STUDY?

Circle the things that you think someone in a **Marine Science Job** might use or study.

Right now, I am _____ years old. This is a picture of me doing a **Marine Science Job**. Right now, this is what I think I might like to do.

BUT I CAN ALWAYS CHANGE MY MIND!

MARKETING
AND
DISTRIBUTION
JOBS

MARKETING AND DISTRIBUTION JOBS
LEADER'S GUIDE

If you are using puppets, select the bear, raccoon, skunk, and Husky dog.

Introduce the lesson by telling the students they will be learning about some jobs that have to do with buying things at stores.

Distribute the student booklets and pencils. Have the students complete the first page. Tell the students that people who make their living buying or selling cars, clothes, toys, furniture, or anything else have jobs in *Marketing and Distribution. Marketing* means buying or selling something. *Distribution* means getting something to people who want it.

Have the students turn to the second page. Read the first part of the page with the students. When naming the four jobs listed on the page, tell the students that they will be learning about these jobs in their booklets.

Then ask the students to name some other jobs that involve *Marketing and Distribution*. Write the appropriate answers on the chalkboard. Some examples could be: *purchasing agent* (buy supplies needed by companies, businesses, schools, churches, etc.), *market researcher* (study what people like and dislike about the products they buy), *credit manager* (decide who can borrow money and how much they can have), *shipping and receiving clerk* (get packages ready for delivery and receive goods coming into a store or business), and *buyer* (buy products and goods from other businesses to sell to other people). If necessary, explain the jobs using the definitions found in the parentheses. Have the students select three *Marketing and Distribution Jobs* and write them on the lines on the page. Read the last sentences on the page with the students.

Tell the students there will be several animal characters in the story and that some of the students will pretend to be the animal characters. (The skunk and raccoon should be boys, and the bear and Husky dog should be girls.) If you are using puppets, give each of the chosen students his/her puppet. Tell these students to sit near you during the lesson and that they will be involved in the story at certain times.

Have the students look at page 3. Read the text with the students. When you have finished reading, ask the following questions:

For the student holding the skunk puppet:

- *Sidney, why were you happy about the modeling job?*

For the rest of the students:

- *How many places can you think of where you would see models?*

Have the students turn to page 4. Read the text with the students. When you have finished reading, ask the following questions:

For the student holding the bear puppet:

- *Bonnie, how do you think your grandmother feels when she has to tell employees that they have done something wrong?*

For the rest of the students:

- *What would be the hardest part of a store manager's job?*
- *What would be the best part of a store manager's job?*

Have the students look at page 5. Read the text with the students. When you have finished reading, ask the following questions:

For the student holding the raccoon puppet:

- *Raul, what could make a salesperson angry?*

For the rest of the students:

- *How many businesses can you name that would need a salesperson?*
- *What would be the hardest thing about being a salesperson?*
- *What would be the best thing about being a salesperson?*

Have the students turn to page 6. Read the text with the students. When you have finished reading, ask the following questions:

For the student holding the Husky dog puppet:

- *Hanna, why would your neighbor have to be in good physical condition to do her job? (Filling shelves would tire her out, and she could not lift the boxes if she wasn't in good physical condition.)*

For the student holding the skunk puppet:

- *Sidney, what was it like to walk around the store in different clothes?*

For the rest of the students:

- *How many different businesses can you name that need someone to stock shelves?*
- *What do you think would be the hardest thing a stock clerk has to do?*
- *What do you think would be the best thing about being a stock clerk?*

If puppets were used in the lesson, collect them from the students.

Give the students crayons or markers and have them complete the activities on pages 7 and 8. If they finish before the allotted time has elapsed, tell them they may color the pictures on other pages.

Conclude the lesson by having the students share their activity pages with the class. Then tell the students they may take their booklets home to share with their parents.

MARKETING AND DISTRIBUTION JOBS

NAME

TEACHER

GRADE

1

There are many jobs that have to do with things we buy. Some of these jobs have to do with getting the merchandise into stores. Other jobs have to do with advertising or selling the products we buy. These are jobs in **Marketing and Distribution.**

Four **Marketing and Distribution Jobs** are:

1. Model

2. Store Manager

3. Salesperson

4. Stock Clerk

Three more **Marketing and Distribution Jobs** are:

1. _____

2. _____

3. _____

In this booklet, a skunk named Sidney is offered a job modeling children's clothes. He meets many different workers who are involved in selling the clothes he will be wearing.

CAREER CRITTERS: MARKETING AND DISTRIBUTION JOBS—STUDENT BOOKLET
© 1996 MAR∗CO PRODUCTS, INC. 1-800-448-2197

I'VE GOT
JUST WHAT YOU NEED

Sidney Skunk has been offered a job modeling children's clothes during a sale at a big department store. Sidney is very happy. All he has to do is wear different clothes while walking around the store. The last time Sidney did this, customers saw Sidney wearing the outfits, liked what they saw, and bought the outfits from a salesperson. Sidney hopes the customers will like what he will be wearing this time, too.

Sidney loves to go to the store. One of the things Sidney likes about the store is that many of the people who work there are related to his friends. The first person Sidney meets at the store is Bonnie Bear's grandmother. She is the store manager, and she is in charge of many things at the store. One of the jobs she does is hire the models and tell them where to work. Bonnie's grandmother takes Sidney to the children's clothing department.

4

When they reach the children's clothing department, Sidney sees someone else he knows. It is Raul Raccoon's father, who is the salesperson.

Raul's father greets Sidney and shows him what to wear and where to get dressed. Raul's father tells Sidney that he expects to sell more clothes today than he has sold in the past month.

CAREER CRITTERS: MARKETING AND DISTRIBUTION JOBS—STUDENT BOOKLET
© 1996 MAR*CO PRODUCTS, INC. 1-800-448-2197

After Sidney dresses in the clothes he is to model, he walks around the children's clothing department. There he sees Hanna Husky's neighbor. She is a stock clerk. She is filling all the shelves with new clothes. She tells Sidney that it will be hard to keep the shelves filled today. The store is expecting many customers during the sale. The closer it gets to the time that the store will open, the more excited Sidney becomes. He can hardly wait to begin his modeling job.

6

WHAT WOULD YOU MODEL?

Complete the picture by drawing the kind of clothes you would like to model.

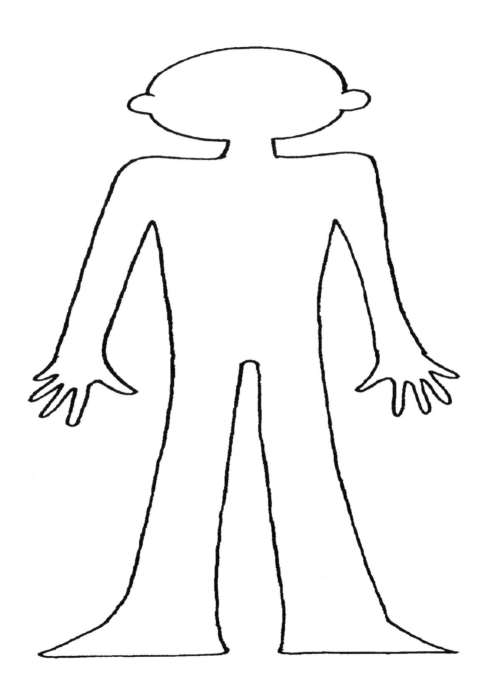

Right now, I am _____ years old. This is a picture of me doing a **Marketing and Distribution Job**. Right now, this is what I think I might like to do.

BUT I CAN ALWAYS CHANGE MY MIND!

PERSONAL SERVICE JOBS

PERSONAL SERVICE JOBS
LEADER'S GUIDE

If you are using puppets, select the donkey, raccoon, skunk, and bear.

Introduce the lesson by telling the students they will be learning about some jobs that help people and make them happy.

Distribute the student booklets and pencils. Have the students complete the first page.

Have the students turn to the second page. Read the first part of the page with the students. When naming the four jobs listed on the page, have the students tell how each helps people.

Then ask the students to name some other jobs that involve *Personal Service*. Write the appropriate answers on the chalkboard. Some examples could be: *airline flight attendant, cook, detective, gas station attendant, hotel clerk, housekeeper, mortician, newspaper carrier, parking lot attendant, dry cleaner.* Have the students select three *Personal-Service Jobs* and write them on the lines on the page. Read the last sentences on the page with the students.

Tell the students there will be several animal characters in the story and that some of the students will pretend to be the animal characters. (The skunk and donkey should be boys, and the raccoon and bear should be girls.) If you are using puppets, give each of the chosen students his/her puppet. Tell these students to sit near you during the lesson and that they will be involved in the story at certain times.

Have the students look at page 3. Read the text with the students. When you have finished reading, ask the following questions:

For the student holding the skunk puppet:

* *Sidney, what were you thinking about when you watched your mom and dad work in the restaurant?*

For the rest of the students:

- *What do people who work in restaurants have to do to make people happy?*
- *If you were going to work in a restaurant, which job would you choose?*
- *If you were going to work in a restaurant, which job would you **not** want?*

Have the students turn to page 4. Read the text with the students. When you have finished reading, ask the following questions:

For the student holding the donkey puppet:

- *Danny, how does your dad help everyone? (by helping to make the town safe to live in)*
- *How do you feel about your dad being a detective?*

For the student holding the skunk puppet:

- *Sidney, why weren't you sure you would want a dangerous job?*

Have the students look at page 5. Read the text with the students. When you have finished reading, ask the following questions:

For the student holding the bear puppet:

- *Bonnie, what do you think your aunt likes most about her job?*
- *What do you think is the hardest thing she has to do?*

For the student holding the skunk puppet:

- *Sidney, do you think most bakers eat some of what they are baking?*

For the student holding the raccoon puppet:

- *Rita, how do you think your grandmother learned to be a repair person?*
- *What do you think made her decide to learn to do this job?*

For the student holding the skunk puppet:

- *Sidney, what show would you miss most if your television set was broken?*

For the rest of the students:

- *If you were going to be a repair person, what would you most like to repair?*
- *What would you like most about being a detective? A baker? A repair person?*
- *What would you **not** like about being a detective? A baker? A repair person?*

Have the students turn to page 6. Read the text with the students. When you have finished reading, ask the following questions:

For the student holding the skunk puppet:

- *Sidney, would you like to be a newspaper carrier? Why? Why not?*

For the rest of the students:

- *What are some jobs that make other people happy?*
- *Would you like to work in a job that makes other people happy?*

If puppets were used in the lesson, collect them from the students.

Give the students crayons or markers and have them complete the activities on pages 7 and 8. If they finish before the allotted time has elapsed, tell them they may color the pictures on other pages.

Conclude the lesson by having the students share their activity pages with the class. Then tell the students they may take their booklets home to share with their parents.

CAREER CRITTERS © MAR*CO PRODUCTS, INC. 1-800-448-2197

PERSONAL SERVICE JOBS

NAME

TEACHER

GRADE

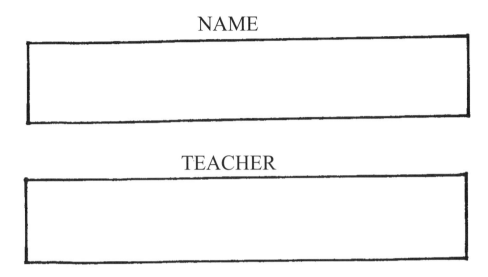

1

Do you feel happy when a waiter or waitress serves you food in a restaurant? Are you glad when a repair person is able to fix your TV set? Jobs like these help people and make them feel better. These are called **Personal Service Jobs**.

Four **Personal Service Jobs** are:

1. Waiter/Waitress

2. Detective

3. Baker

4. Repair Person

Three more **Personal Service Jobs** are:

1. _____

2. _____

3. _____

Sidney Skunk likes making people happy. In this booklet, he explores different jobs that do just that.

CAREER CRITTERS: PERSONAL SERVICE JOBS—STUDENT BOOKLET
© 1996 MAR*CO PRODUCTS, INC. 1-800-448-2197

MAKING PEOPLE HAPPY

Sidney Skunk sat quietly in a corner of his parents' restaurant. The Carrot Patch was the most popular restaurant in Animaltown. Sidney thought his parents were the best cooks and waiters in the world.

It was six o'clock at night, and almost every stool was filled. Dad was taking orders and serving food. Mom was cooking. Sometimes they switched jobs. Then Mom would serve the customers and Dad would cook.

Sidney's parents make people happy. Sidney thinks that is nice. When he grows up, he might work in the restaurant or do other things to help people and make them happy.

He could be a detective like Danny Donkey's dad. Without detectives, many crimes would not be solved, and people who did bad things would not get caught. Danny's dad helps everybody because he helps make Animaltown a safe place to live. Of course, his job could be dangerous. Sidney wasn't so sure that he wanted a dangerous job.

4

Maybe he would be a baker, like Bonnie Bear's aunt. Now *there* was a job that made people happy! Those cakes and cookies really put a smile on people's faces. He wondered if bakers could eat all the cakes and cookies they wanted without paying for them.

Or maybe he could be a repair person. Rita Raccoon's grandmother repaired television sets, and that *really* made people happy. No one likes not being able to see their favorite shows.

More and more jobs kept popping into Sidney's mind. He could be a flight attendant on an airplane and travel all over the world. He could be a hair stylist and make men and women look good. Maybe working in a parking lot would be fun. He can run fast, and he sure would like driving all those cars. Of course, he would have to grow up before he could do most of those things. As a kid, though, he could be a newspaper carrier. That's a job that helps people, too.

CAREER CRITTERS: PERSONAL SERVICE JOBS—STUDENT BOOKLET
© 1996 MAR✳CO PRODUCTS, INC. 1-800-448-2197

HOW I WOULD FEEL

Look at the three faces. One is smiling, another is sad, and the third is neither smiling or sad. It's just so-so. Draw a line from the picture of each worker to the face that shows how you would feel doing that job.

CAREER CRITTERS: PERSONAL SERVICE JOBS—STUDENT BOOKLET
© 1996 MAR∗CO PRODUCTS, INC. 1-800-448-2197

Right now, I am _____ years old. This is a picture of me doing a **Personal Service Job**. Right now, this is what I think I might like to do.

BUT I CAN ALWAYS CHANGE MY MIND!

PUBLIC SERVICE JOBS

PUBLIC SERVICE JOBS
LEADER'S GUIDE

If you are using puppets, select the bear, squirrel, raccoon, and skunk.

Introduce the lesson by telling the students they will be learning about some jobs that help people.

Distribute the student booklets and pencils. Have the students complete the first page. Tell the students that people who make a living delivering mail, fighting fires, doing police work, and discovering new places are said to have jobs in *Public Service*.

Have the students turn to the second page. Read the first part of the page with the students. When naming the four jobs listed on the page, have the students tell how each does something for people.

Then ask the students to name some other jobs that involve *Public Service*. Write the appropriate answers on the chalkboard. Some examples could be: *police officer, bank clerk, garbage collector, social worker*. Have the students select three *Public Service Jobs* and write them on the lines on the page. Read the last sentence on the page with the students.

Tell the students there will be several animal characters in the story and that some of the students will pretend to be the animal characters. (The bear and raccoon should be boys, and the skunk and squirrel should be girls.) If you are using puppets, give each of the chosen students his/her puppet. Tell these students to sit near you during the lesson and that they will be involved in the story at certain times.

Have the students look at page 3. Read the text with the students. When you have finished reading, ask the following questions:

For the student holding the bear puppet:

- *Bono, why did you think you could be a mail carrier?*

For the student holding the raccoon puppet:

- *Raul, how do you think your uncle feels when it rains?*

For the rest of the students:

- *How many different jobs can you name that have to do with mail?*
- *What would be the hardest thing about being a mail carrier?*
- *What would be the best thing about being a mail carrier?*

Have the students turn to page 4. Read the text together. When you have finished reading, ask the following questions:

For the student holding the bear puppet:

- *Bono, what was the first thing that came to your mind when you heard the siren?*

For the rest of the students:

- *How many jobs can you name that have to do with fighting fires?*
- *What would be the hardest thing about being a firefighter?*
- *What would be the best thing about being a firefighter?*

Have the students look at page 5. Read the text with the students. When you have finished reading, ask the following questions:

For the student holding the skunk puppet:

- *Selena, what makes you think so highly of your music teacher?*

For the student holding the bear puppet:

- *Bono, why did you think you might like to be a music teacher?*

For the rest of the students:

- *How many jobs can you name that have to do with teaching?*
- *What would be the hardest thing about being a teacher?*
- *What would be the best thing about being a teacher?*

Have the students turn to page 6. Read the text with the students. When you have finished reading, ask the following questions:

For the student holding the squirrel puppet:

- *Shanna, how do astronauts help people?*

For the student holding the bear puppet:

- *Bono, why would you like to be an astronaut?*

For the rest of the students:

- *How many jobs can you name that have to do with space flight?*
- *What would be the hardest thing about being an astronaut?*
- *What would be the best thing about being an astronaut?*

If puppets were used in the lesson, collect them from the students.

Give the students crayons or markers and have them complete the activities on pages 7 and 8. If they finish before the allotted time has elapsed, tell them they may color the pictures on other pages.

Conclude the lesson by having the students share their activity pages with the class. Then tell the students they may take their booklets home to share with their parents.

PUBLIC SERVICE JOBS

NAME

TEACHER

GRADE

1

A house is on fire, and a fire truck speeds down the street. A letter is mailed, and someone delivers it. A space shuttle blasts off to explore space. A teacher helps a student learn. These and other jobs have to do with working to provide everyone with a better life. These are **Public Service Jobs**.

Four **Public Service Jobs** are:

1. Mail Carrier

2. Astronaut

3. Firefighter

4. Music Teacher

Three more **Public Service Jobs** are:

1. _____

2. _____

3. _____

In this booklet, Bono Bear thinks he would like to have a **Public Service Job** and do something to make life better for other people.

CAREER CRITTERS: PUBLIC SERVICE JOBS—STUDENT BOOKLET
© 1996 MAR✳CO PRODUCTS, INC. 1-800-448-2197

MAKING LIFE BETTER

Bono Bear loves to play outside. While he was playing one day, he saw Raul Raccoon's uncle delivering the mail. Raul had told Bono that you need to move quickly to deliver the mail. As Bono watched Raul's uncle, he knew Raul was right. Raul's uncle moved quickly from house to house. Bono thought, "I'm fast. I could be a mail carrier."

CAREER CRITTERS: PUBLIC SERVICE JOBS—STUDENT BOOKLET
© 1996 MAR∗CO PRODUCTS, INC. 1-800-448-2197

Bono was running around his front yard. He was pretending he was a mail carrier. Suddenly, he heard a loud siren. He looked down the street to see a fire truck rushing toward his house.

As the fire truck sped past Bono's house, down the street, and off into the distance, Bono knew that there must be a fire somewhere. The firefighters were coming to the rescue. Bono thought, "I would like to be a firefighter and come to the rescue."

CAREER CRITTERS: PUBLIC SERVICE JOBS—STUDENT BOOKLET
© 1996 MAR✳CO PRODUCTS, INC. 1-800-448-2197

Bono Bear was tired of playing outside, so he went into his house to rest. The phone rang. It was Selena Skunk. She had just finished her music lesson. She told Bono how much she loved music, and that her teacher was the best in the world. Bono loved music, too. He thought about how great it would be to play and teach music and be admired by his students.

Bono finished talking with Selena, then sat down to watch TV. A special report came on. Shanna Squirrel was talking about her mother, the astronaut who had just returned from a mission to outer space. Shanna said that she would like to be an astronaut. Bono thought he would love to be an astronaut, too. He thought about how the jobs he'd seen that day helped make life better. Bono liked the idea of having a job that made life better.

6

WHAT DO I NEED?

Draw a line from the worker to something the worker uses.

Right now, I am _____ years old. This is a picture of me doing a **Public Service Job**. Right now, this is what I think I might like to do.

BUT I CAN ALWAYS CHANGE MY MIND!

TRANSPORTATION JOBS

TRANSPORTATION JOBS
LEADER'S GUIDE

If you are using puppets, select the donkey, Husky dog, raccoon, and bear.

Introduce the lesson by telling the students they will be learning about some jobs that require people to travel.

Distribute the student booklets and pencils. Have the students complete the first page. Tell the students that people who make their living delivering things or helping people or things get from place to place have jobs in *Transportation*.

Have the students turn to the second page. Read the first part of the page with the students. When naming the four jobs listed on the page, have the students tell how each has something to do with travel.

Then ask the students to name some other jobs that involve *Transportation*. Write the appropriate answers on the chalkboard. Some examples could be: *train engineer, taxi driver, bus driver, ship's captain, air traffic controller.* Have the students select three *Transportation Jobs* and write them on the lines on the page. Read the last sentence on the page with the students.

Tell the students there will be several animal characters in the story and that some of the students will pretend to be the animal characters. (The Husky dog and donkey should be boys, and the raccoon and bear should be girls.) If you are using puppets, give each of the chosen students his/her puppet. Tell these students to sit near you during the lesson and that they will be involved in the story at certain times.

Have the students look at page 3. Read the text with the students. When you have finished reading, ask the following questions:

For the student holding the Husky dog puppet:

- *Hanuk, what might a sled carry? (clothing, food, tools, building supplies, etc.)*

For the rest of the students:

- *How many different jobs can you name that have to do with ice and snow?*
- *What would be the hardest thing about driving a dog sled?*
- *What would be the best thing about driving a dog sled?*

Have the students turn to page 4. Read the text with the students. When you have finished reading, ask the following questions:

For the student holding the raccoon puppet:

- *Rita, what might your uncle carry in his truck?*

For the student holding the Husky dog puppet:

- *Hanuk, why would you like to drive a truck?*

For the rest of the students:

- *What would be the most important things to do when driving a truck? (keep your eyes on the road, obey the speed limit, etc.)*
- *What would be the best thing about driving a truck?*

Have the students look at page 5. Read the text with the students. When you have finished reading, ask the following questions:

For the student holding the donkey puppet:

- *Danny, does your neighbor mind being away from home for long periods of time? (Ships can be at sea for months, so a sailor must not mind being away from home for a long time.)*

For the student holding the Husky dog puppet:

- *Hanuk, if you were a sailor, where would you like to go?*

For the rest of the students:

- *How many jobs can you name that have something to do with ships?*
- *What would be the hardest thing about being a sailor?*
- *What would be the best thing about being a sailor?*

Have the students turn to page 6. Read the text with the students. When you have finished reading, ask the following questions:

For the student holding the bear puppet:

- *Bonnie, what did your aunt have to do before she could become a pilot? (take lessons, pass a test, and get a license)*

For the student holding the Husky dog puppet:

- *Hanuk, how do you think you would feel if you were piloting a plane 35,000 feet above the ground?*

For the rest of the students:

- *How many jobs can you name that have to do with airplanes?*
- *Why must pilots always be alert?*
- *Why must pilots be able to think quickly in emergency situations?*

If puppets were used in the lesson, collect them from the students.

Give the students crayons or markers and have them complete the activities on pages 7 and 8. If they finish before the allotted time has elapsed, tell them they may color the pictures on other pages.

Conclude the lesson by having the students share their activity pages with the class. Then tell the students they may take their booklets home to share with their parents.

TRANSPORTATION JOBS

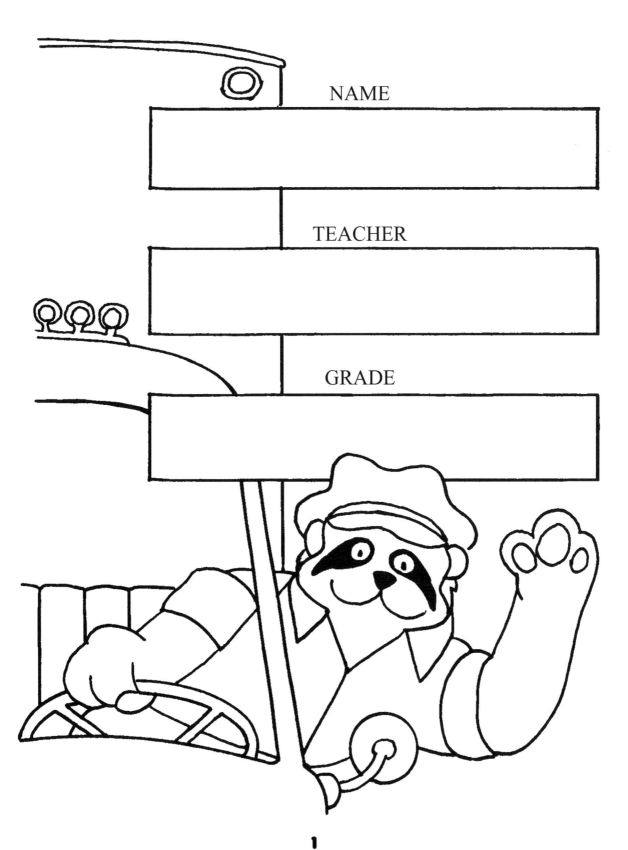

NAME

TEACHER

GRADE

1

There are many jobs that have to do with moving people or things from place to place. People who work in these jobs may use airplanes, buses, trains, trucks, sleds, or ships. These are jobs in **Transportation**.

Four **Transportation Jobs** are:

1. Dog Sled Driver

2. Truck Driver

3. Sailor

4. Pilot

Three more **Transportation Jobs** are:

1. _____

2. _____

3. _____

In this booklet, a Husky puppy named Hanuk dreams of having different kinds of **Transportation Jobs**.

HOW DOES IT GET THERE?

Hanuk is a Husky puppy. He lives in a snowy village in Alaska. Hanuk knows that Huskies are important dogs with an important job. You see, Hanuk's parents are sled dogs. Hanuk's parents pull sleds filled with important things to faraway places, where the things are needed by others. Hanuk dreams that one day he will be a sled dog, pulling a sled filled with important things and taking them to faraway places.

One day, Hanuk sees Rita Raccoon. Her uncle is a truck driver. This very day, Rita's uncle is driving a truck filled with important things to the big city. Rita says that a truck cannot drive on the snow, like a dog sled. A truck needs a road.

Rita's uncle sees Hanuk looking at the truck and asks him to come along for the ride. As they are driving down the road, Hanuk imagines himself being a truck driver and driving a big truck filled with important things to the city.

When Hanuk and Rita's uncle reach the city, they drive to a place called *the docks*. The truck is unloaded, and the things from inside the truck are put on a big ship. At the dock, Hanuk meets Danny Donkey. Danny has come to the docks to visit his neighbor, who is a sailor on one of the ships. He is away from home for long periods of time when the ship he works on carries important things across the ocean. As Hanuk rides home, he dreams of being a sailor on a ship filled with important things.

Back in his village, Hanuk is staring up at the sky. He is daydreaming about the different jobs he can have when he grows up. As he is thinking, he notices a big, shiny, birdlike thing in the sky. Hanuk's friend, Bonnie Bear, tells him that the shiny thing is an airplane. Bonnie says her aunt is a pilot who flies airplanes carrying many important things to faraway places. Hanuk looks up at the sky and begins to imagine he is piloting the plane to a place he has never seen. As the plane fades from his view, Hanuk wonders which of the jobs he will be able to do.

6

WHERE WOULD YOU FIND ME?

Draw a line to match the pictures.

Right now, I am _____ years old. This is a picture of me doing a **Transportation Job**. Right now, this is what I think I might like to do.

BUT I CAN ALWAYS CHANGE MY MIND!

STICK-PUPPET
PATTERNS

These simple stick puppets are easy to make.

1. Reproduce the pattern.

2. Glue the pattern onto cardboard or heavyweight paper. Cut the pattern outline along the heavy line.

3. Color the puppet. You may also decorate the shape with yarn, glitter, fabric, etc.

4. Optional: Laminate the puppet for greater durability.

5. Glue a craft stick/paint stirrer onto the back of your completed stick puppet.

CAREER CRITTERS © MAR*CO PRODUCTS, INC. 1-800-448-2197

193

TICKET

195

196

Today
IS
Career
Awareness
Day!

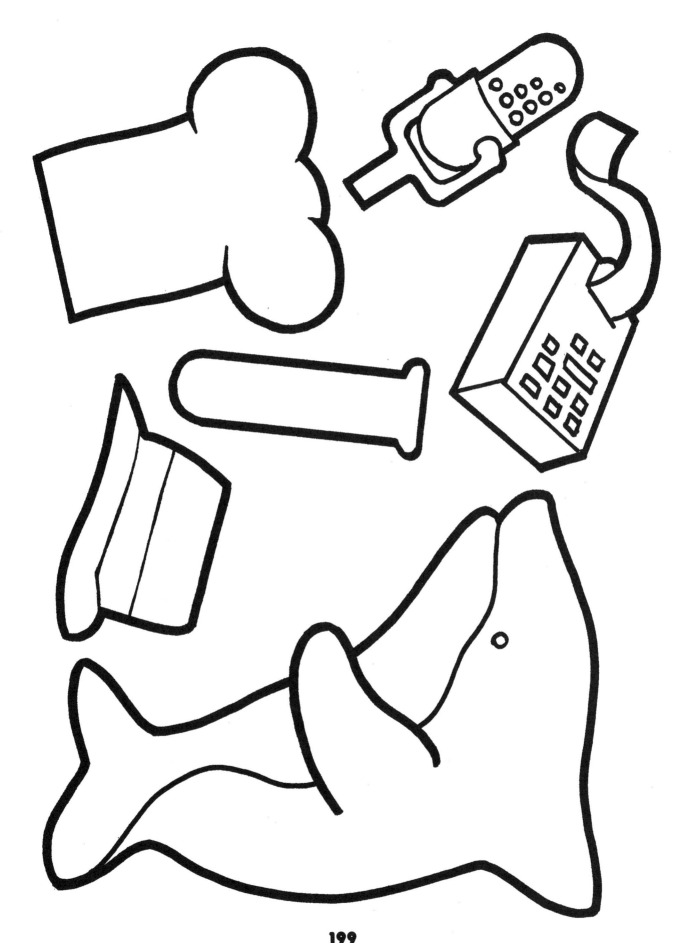

199

CAREER-AWARENESS MATERIALS AVAILABLE FROM
MAR*CO PRODUCTS, INC.

1-2-3 Careers for Me (Preschool-Grade 1)
Alphabet Careers (Grades 2-4)
Career Bingo I Game (Preschool-Grade 3)
Career Bingo II Game (Grades 4-8)
Career Fun Gamekit (Grades 1-5)
Career Pay Day Game (Grades 4-12)
Careers I Know Bingo Game (Grades 4-8)
Me and My Job (Grades 2-4)
Picture Me This! Game (Grades 1-6)
Rappin' Up Careers (Grades 4-8)
What Could I Be? Gamekit (Grades 2-5)